Your Legacy Protection Plan

A Simple Guide to Life Insurance, Family Protection, and Future Planning

Kayla Price

Licensed Insurance Professional

This book is intended for educational and informational purposes only. It is not a substitute for professional legal, tax, financial, insurance, medical, Medicare, Medicaid, Social Security, retirement, or investment advice. Rules, costs, program details, product availability, and annual figures may change. Always verify current information with the appropriate qualified professional before making decisions.

For additional educational resources, visit:

priceservicesgroup.com

Price Services Group, L.L.C.

info@priceservicesgroup.com | 1-866-648-1578

Printed in the United States of America. First Edition, 2026

Important Disclaimer

This guide is for educational purposes only. It is not legal, tax, investment, financial, estate planning, insurance, or retirement advice.

Nothing in this guide creates an attorney-client relationship unless separately agreed in writing. Readers should consult qualified professionals before making decisions.

Life insurance product availability, underwriting, premiums, riders, exclusions, limitations, and guarantees vary by carrier, product, state, and individual eligibility.

Insurance and annuity guarantees are based on the financial strength and claims-paying ability of the issuing carrier.

Cash value life insurance may involve fees, surrender charges, loan interest, tax consequences, and policy lapse risk. Policy loans and withdrawals may reduce cash value and death benefit.

Examples are hypothetical and educational only. Price Services Group, L.L.C. is not affiliated with or endorsed by any government agency.

A Note Before You Begin

Protection planning is not about fear. It is about clarity, family stability, and choices.

Many people delay the conversation because they assume it will be confusing, expensive, or uncomfortable. This book was written to make the subject easier to approach. You do not need to know every insurance term before asking good questions. You do not need to have a perfect budget before exploring what is possible. You simply need a clear starting point.

Kayla Price and Price Services Group, L.L.C. believe the planning conversation should begin with the person, the household, and the purpose. That is the heart of the phrase Where You Matter.

How to Use This Book

Read this book with a pen nearby. Circle what sounds familiar. Mark what feels uncertain. Make a note when a chapter describes a decision you have been avoiding or a question your family has never discussed.

This is not intended to be a do-it-yourself manual. It is a guide to help you understand the language of protection planning before you sit down for a personalized review.

If you would like help reviewing your current coverage, retirement income plan, life insurance, or protection gaps, you can schedule a personalized conversation: https://host.safemsngr.com/widget/bookings/psglifeandretirementplan

Table of Contents

Chapter One

Protecting What Matters Most

Building a foundation for family protection and legacy.

KAYLA PRICE

Chapter 1: Protection Planning Without the Pressure

Why This Matters Now

Most people do not ask for protection planning because they want another bill. They ask because they want a calmer way to think about responsibility, love, debt, income, and the people who would have to keep going if life changed suddenly.

In a healthy planning conversation, clarity instead of pressure is the starting point. The goal is not to make anyone anxious or to make a product sound perfect. The goal is to understand what the coverage is supposed to protect, how long that need may last, and what tradeoffs are reasonable for the household.

Protection planning is not about fear. It is about giving the people you love more room to breathe if income, health, debt, business responsibilities, or family needs change unexpectedly.

A policy may be part of the answer, but the policy should follow the purpose. Clear goals make the product conversation calmer, more useful, and easier to review over time.

The Simple Explanation

At its simplest, protection planning without the pressure is about what should remain possible for the family if life changes suddenly. That does not mean every solution is simple. It means the purpose can be stated in ordinary language before the details begin.

Life insurance products are contracts, so premiums, underwriting, riders, exclusions, limitations, state availability, and policy terms all matter. The details should support the family goal instead of overwhelming it.

Some coverage is designed to last for a specific period. Some coverage is designed to last longer if premiums are paid and the policy stays in force. Some policies may build cash value. Some

may include riders that can help during qualifying illness events. Some products are built for protection only, while others may cross into retirement income, safe money, or legacy conversations.

Aisha and Marcus are raising two children, paying a mortgage, and helping an aging parent. They do not want a dramatic sales conversation. They want someone to slow the discussion down and show where the gaps may be.

A Client-Style Scenario

In an early conversation, it is normal not to know which type of coverage belongs in the discussion. The review should begin with the need, then narrow the options from there.

The better question is not simply what can be purchased today. The better question is what problem the coverage is supposed to solve and how the family would actually use it later.

One common misunderstanding is that pressure, fear, and speed are signs that a plan is stronger. This belief can cause people to either delay planning or overcorrect with a decision that does not fit.

What Gets Misunderstood

Another misunderstanding is that protection planning without the pressure can be judged by one feature alone. People may focus only on premium, only on cash value, only on the death benefit, only on a rider, or only on a story they heard from someone else. Those details matter, but they need context.

Another common mistake is assuming the planning is finished once a policy is placed. Life changes, employer benefits change, beneficiaries become outdated, and some policies need attention to stay aligned with the original goal.

What people often overlook with protection planning without the pressure is the family conversation around it. Someone may need to know where documents are kept, who to call, what the intended purpose is, and whether there are special family dynamics to consider.

What Often Gets Missed

Ownership and beneficiary choices deserve careful attention. The policy owner controls the contract, the insured is the person covered, and the beneficiary receives the death benefit if the policy pays.

Timing also matters. Waiting can affect insurability, premium, and available options, while moving too quickly can create regret if the policy does not match the goal.

A protection review usually looks at current coverage, income needs, debts, dependents, timing, budget, and decision comfort. It may also compare existing coverage with current goals and identify gaps that are not obvious from policy pages alone.

Inside a Thoughtful Review

A review may include income replacement, final expenses, mortgage protection, children, aging parents, business obligations, retirement timing, health considerations, and beneficiary updates.

The review should also ask what you do not want. Some people want temporary low-cost coverage, some want lifelong protection, some want to explore cash value carefully, and some want to avoid complexity.

If this sounds like your situation, mark the section and bring your questions to a protection review.

Chapter Summary

The main lesson of this chapter is that protection planning without the pressure should be discussed with patience and context. A policy is only useful when it supports the real-life purpose behind it.

There is no single answer that fits every family. The right conversation considers need, time horizon, budget, health, product design, and future review.

As you continue, keep asking one simple question: what would this coverage help my family preserve, avoid, or complete?

Next Conversation

The next chapter turns to what life insurance is really for, continuing the same theme: protection planning works best when the product discussion follows the human need.

A Calmer Way to Begin

A strong review can start with ordinary questions: who depends on you, what bills would continue, what would be emotionally hardest for the family to manage, and what decisions should not have to be made in a rush. When clients are given room to answer honestly, the conversation becomes more useful. The goal is not to scare anyone into action. It is to help a family see where clarity would be a gift.

Price Services Group can serve as a guide in that process by organizing the conversation, explaining options, and helping the client decide what deserves attention first.

Questions to Bring to a No-Pressure Review

What would I want my family to be able to decide calmly? Which bills would create pressure first? Who would help my spouse, children, parents, or business if I could not? What coverage do I already have, and what do I not understand about it? These questions are enough to begin.

What Pressure-Free Planning Sounds Like

A pressure-free conversation has a different rhythm. It does not begin with a product sheet. It begins with the client saying what has changed, what feels uncertain, and what they want their family to be able to decide calmly. One person may say, "I just bought a house and do not know if my work coverage is enough." Another may say, "My parents are aging and I am starting to think differently about my own children." Another may say, "I have policies, but I do not know what they mean."

Those are not small questions. They are the real doorway into planning. When the conversation is respectful, the client does not have to pretend to be more certain than they are. They can ask what a rider means, why underwriting matters, why a beneficiary form should be reviewed, or whether a quote is truly affordable.

The best next step is often simple. Gather what you have, name what changed, and let the review sort the order of priorities. That may lead to term coverage, permanent coverage, final expense planning, living benefits, business protection, or no immediate change at all. The value is the clarity.

The Value of Not Waiting for Perfect Timing

People often wait for the perfect moment to review coverage, but family protection rarely becomes easier by ignoring it. A review does not require a perfect budget, perfect paperwork, or perfect certainty. It only requires a willingness to look honestly at what has changed and what loved ones may need. That small act of attention can prevent years of assumptions from becoming tomorrow's confusion.

The most useful review is often the one that finally puts names to vague concerns. Once the concern has a name, the next step can be discussed calmly, with enough context to decide whether coverage should change or simply be better understood.

Reflection for Your Notes

As you think about protection planning without the pressure, write down what feels settled and what still feels unclear. A protection review is not about proving that you already know the answer. It is about bringing the right questions into the room so the next step is based on your life, your people, your budget, and your priorities.

Chapter 2: What Life Insurance Is Really For

The Real-Life Reason

Life insurance is often described as a death benefit, but families experience it as time, choices, and breathing room. It can give survivors a way to pay bills, keep promises, settle immediate costs, and avoid making every decision from a place of panic.

In a healthy planning conversation, money arriving when a family needs choices is the starting point. The goal is not to make anyone anxious or to make a product sound perfect. The goal is to understand what the coverage is supposed to protect, how long that need may last, and what tradeoffs are reasonable for the household.

Protection planning is not about fear. It is about giving the people you love more room to breathe if income, health, debt, business responsibilities, or family needs change unexpectedly.

A policy may be part of the answer, but the policy should follow the purpose. Clear goals make the product conversation calmer, more useful, and easier to review over time.

Plain English First

At its simplest, what life insurance is really for is about replacing options that would otherwise disappear. That does not mean every solution is simple. It means the purpose can be stated in ordinary language before the details begin.

Life insurance products are contracts, so premiums, underwriting, riders, exclusions, limitations, state availability, and policy terms all matter. The details should support the family goal instead of overwhelming it.

Some coverage is designed to last for a specific period. Some coverage is designed to last longer if premiums are paid and the policy stays in force. Some policies may build cash value. Some may include riders that can help during qualifying illness events.

Some products are built for protection only, while others may cross into retirement income, safe money, or legacy conversations.

Denise carries coverage through work and assumes that means her family is set. When she changes jobs, she learns the coverage may not travel with her.

How This Can Show Up

In an early conversation, it is normal not to know which type of coverage belongs in the discussion. The review should begin with the need, then narrow the options from there.

The better question is not simply what can be purchased today. The better question is what problem the coverage is supposed to solve and how the family would actually use it later.

One common misunderstanding is that life insurance is only for burial or only for people with children. This belief can cause people to either delay planning or overcorrect with a decision that does not fit.

A Common Misread

Another misunderstanding is that what life insurance is really for can be judged by one feature alone. People may focus only on premium, only on cash value, only on the death benefit, only on a rider, or only on a story they heard from someone else. Those details matter, but they need context.

Another common mistake is assuming the planning is finished once a policy is placed. Life changes, employer benefits change, beneficiaries become outdated, and some policies need attention to stay aligned with the original goal.

What people often overlook with what life insurance is really for is the family conversation around it. Someone may need to know where documents are kept, who to call, what the intended purpose is, and whether there are special family dynamics to consider.

The Quiet Details

Ownership and beneficiary choices deserve careful attention. The policy owner controls the contract, the insured is the person covered, and the beneficiary receives the death benefit if the policy pays.

Timing also matters. Waiting can affect insurability, premium, and available options, while moving too quickly can create regret if the policy does not match the goal.

A protection review usually looks at who depends on the insured, what expenses continue, what goals should survive, and how long support may be needed. It may also compare existing coverage with current goals and identify gaps that are not obvious from policy pages alone.

What an Advisor Looks For

A review may include income replacement, final expenses, mortgage protection, children, aging parents, business obligations, retirement timing, health considerations, and beneficiary updates.

The review should also ask what you do not want. Some people want temporary low-cost coverage, some want lifelong protection, some want to explore cash value carefully, and some want to avoid complexity.

If this sounds like your situation, mark the section and bring your questions to a protection review.

In Short

The main lesson of this chapter is that what life insurance is really for should be discussed with patience and context. A policy is only useful when it supports the real-life purpose behind it.

There is no single answer that fits every family. The right conversation considers need, time horizon, budget, health, product design, and future review.

As you continue, keep asking one simple question: what would this coverage help my family preserve, avoid, or complete?

A Soft Step Forward

The next chapter turns to the difference between term and permanent life insurance, continuing the same theme: protection planning works best when the product discussion follows the human need.

What the Money Is Really Buying

When a family receives life insurance proceeds, the check does not grieve for them, make decisions for them, or replace the person they lost. What it can do is create room. It may let a surviving spouse take time away from work, keep children in the same school, pay for help around the house, or avoid selling assets under pressure.

That is why a review should look beyond the funeral. Final costs matter, but so do the months and years after the service. Rent or mortgage payments continue. Utilities continue. Groceries continue. Child care, transportation, insurance premiums, medical bills, and taxes may continue. The family may also have dreams that should not disappear immediately, such as college plans, caring for a parent, or keeping a business stable.

A helpful way to think about life insurance is to name the job of the money. One part may be for immediate expenses. Another part may be for survivor income. Another may be for debt. Another may be for children or legacy. When every dollar has a job, the coverage amount becomes less random.

Review Questions for This Chapter

A thoughtful review may ask who would be financially affected by your death, how quickly they would need cash, what income would stop, what debts would remain, and which family goals should still have a chance. It may also ask whether employer coverage is portable, whether beneficiaries are current, and whether the amount you own still matches your life today.

A More Personal Way to Estimate Need

Instead of starting with a round number, name the promises. Would you want a spouse to have one year of transition time, several years of income, the mortgage paid, college protected, final expenses handled, or business debt resolved? The answer may not be perfect, but it is more meaningful than guessing.

The Survivor Income Question

One of the clearest ways to understand life insurance is to imagine the income conversation after a loss. If one paycheck stops, what happens in the first month? What happens in the first year? What happens when children need school supplies, a car needs repair, the mortgage is due, or a surviving spouse needs time to grieve before making major decisions?

Survivor income is not always about replacing every dollar forever. It may be about creating a bridge. For a young family, that bridge may need to last many years. For a near-retiree, it may need to protect a spouse until retirement income sources are organized. For a business owner, it may need to give the family time while the business is sold, transitioned, or stabilized.

This is why life insurance should be reviewed after major life events. Marriage changes responsibilities. Divorce changes beneficiaries and financial assumptions. A new child changes the timeline. A home purchase adds a debt that may outlive one income. A death in the family can reveal how confusing paperwork becomes when nobody planned ahead. A review turns those life changes into practical questions rather than vague worry.

What a Benefit Can Protect Emotionally

There is an emotional side to the death benefit that families often understand only after they have watched someone else go through a loss. Money cannot remove grief, but it can reduce the number of financial decisions attached to grief. It can keep a surviving spouse from having to choose immediately between returning to work and being present for children. It can give adult children time to settle final matters without arguing over who pays which bill. It can help a family avoid using credit cards, draining emergency savings, or selling a home before they are ready.

That is why the review should include both numbers and feelings. The numbers tell the advisor what is measurable: income, debts, savings, expenses, and time horizon. The feelings reveal what the family most wants to protect: stability, privacy, independence, dignity, education, the home, or the ability to make decisions slowly. Both kinds of information matter.

When clients understand life insurance this way, the conversation becomes less about buying a policy and more about designing a cushion for the people they love.

When Coverage Is Too Small for the Real Need

Many people have some life insurance, but the question is whether it is enough for the job assigned to it. A small workplace benefit may help with immediate costs but may not replace income. A policy bought years ago may have made sense before children, a mortgage, or a business loan. A policy intended for final expenses may not be built to protect survivor income.

This is why Kayla may ask what each policy is supposed to do. If the answer is unclear, the review can rename the purpose. One policy may be for burial and immediate expenses. Another may be for the mortgage. Another may be for spouse income. Another may be for a business agreement. Naming the job helps reveal whether the amount, duration, and beneficiary still make sense.

Reflection for Your Notes

As you think about what life insurance is really for, write down what feels settled and what still feels unclear. A protection review is not about proving that you already know the answer. It is about bringing the right questions into the room so the next step is based on your life, your people, your budget, and your priorities.

Chapter 3: The Difference Between Term and Permanent Life Insurance

Start With the Human Need

The term-versus-permanent question can feel bigger than it needs to be. A clearer way to begin is to ask how long the need lasts, what the policy is supposed to do, and whether the family needs temporary protection, lifelong protection, or a careful blend of both.

In a healthy planning conversation, matching duration to purpose is the starting point. The goal is not to make anyone anxious or to make a product sound perfect. The goal is to understand what the coverage is supposed to protect, how long that need may last, and what tradeoffs are reasonable for the household.

Protection planning is not about fear. It is about giving the people you love more room to breathe if income, health, debt, business responsibilities, or family needs change unexpectedly.

A policy may be part of the answer, but the policy should follow the purpose. Clear goals make the product conversation calmer, more useful, and easier to review over time.

How the Concept Works

At its simplest, the difference between term and permanent life insurance is about choosing coverage that fits the length of the need. That does not mean every solution is simple. It means the purpose can be stated in ordinary language before the details begin.

Life insurance products are contracts, so premiums, underwriting, riders, exclusions, limitations, state availability, and policy terms all matter. The details should support the family goal instead of overwhelming it.

Some coverage is designed to last for a specific period. Some coverage is designed to last longer if premiums are paid and the

policy stays in force. Some policies may build cash value. Some may include riders that can help during qualifying illness events. Some products are built for protection only, while others may cross into retirement income, safe money, or legacy conversations.

A young couple uses term coverage for the mortgage years while also discussing whether modest permanent coverage has a place for final expenses later.

Important Nuance

Term life insurance is often used for needs with a defined time period. Examples include income replacement while children are young, mortgage years, business debt, or a period before retirement savings are fully built. Term can be efficient because it focuses on death benefit protection for a selected period rather than lifelong guarantees or cash value.

Permanent life insurance is designed to remain in force for life when premiums are paid as required and the policy stays in force. Permanent policies can include whole life, universal life, indexed universal life, and other designs. They may include cash value features, flexible funding structures, or guarantees depending on the product.

A common planning approach is not either-or. Some families use term coverage for the large temporary risk and permanent coverage for a smaller lifelong need such as final expenses, legacy intentions, or long-term planning flexibility.

A Familiar Situation

In an early conversation, it is normal not to know which type of coverage belongs in the discussion. The review should begin with the need, then narrow the options from there.

The better question is not simply what can be purchased today. The better question is what problem the coverage is supposed to solve and how the family would actually use it later.

One common misunderstanding is that one type of life insurance is always better than the other. This belief can cause people to either delay planning or overcorrect with a decision that does not fit.

Where Confusion Begins

Another misunderstanding is that the difference between term and permanent life insurance can be judged by one feature alone. People may focus only on premium, only on cash value, only on the death benefit, only on a rider, or only on a story they heard from someone else. Those details matter, but they need context.

Another common mistake is assuming the planning is finished once a policy is placed. Life changes, employer benefits change, beneficiaries become outdated, and some policies need attention to stay aligned with the original goal.

What people often overlook with the difference between term and permanent life insurance is the family conversation around it. Someone may need to know where documents are kept, who to call, what the intended purpose is, and whether there are special family dynamics to consider.

The Overlooked Pieces

Ownership and beneficiary choices deserve careful attention. The policy owner controls the contract, the insured is the person covered, and the beneficiary receives the death benefit if the policy pays.

Timing also matters. Waiting can affect insurability, premium, and available options, while moving too quickly can create regret if the policy does not match the goal.

A protection review usually looks at coverage period, affordability, health, future conversion options, cash value goals, and long-range family intentions. It may also compare existing coverage with current goals and identify gaps that are not obvious from policy pages alone.

Review Questions to Bring Forward

A review may include income replacement, final expenses, mortgage protection, children, aging parents, business obligations, retirement timing, health considerations, and beneficiary updates.

The review should also ask what you do not want. Some people want temporary low-cost coverage, some want lifelong protection, some want to explore cash value carefully, and some want to avoid complexity.

If this sounds like your situation, mark the section and bring your questions to a protection review.

The Main Point

The main lesson of this chapter is that the difference between term and permanent life insurance should be discussed with patience and context. A policy is only useful when it supports the real-life purpose behind it.

There is no single answer that fits every family. The right conversation considers need, time horizon, budget, health, product design, and future review.

As you continue, keep asking one simple question: what would this coverage help my family preserve, avoid, or complete?

Looking Ahead

The next chapter turns to final expense and end-of-life cost planning, continuing the same theme: protection planning works best when the product discussion follows the human need.

Matching the Tool to the Timeline

A temporary need often calls for a temporary conversation. A young family may need a larger amount of death benefit while children are dependent and the mortgage is high. A lifelong need may call for a different discussion, especially when final expenses, legacy goals, or long-term family support are part of the picture.

The review should not force a choice before the need is clear. Sometimes term coverage, permanent coverage, or a combination may be reviewed. The best fit depends on duration, budget, health, and purpose.

A Blended Example

Consider a couple in their thirties with two children and a new mortgage. Their largest risk is temporary: if one parent dies during the child-raising years, the surviving parent may need significant income support. Term life may be reviewed for that large temporary need because it can provide a larger death benefit for a defined period at a lower initial premium than many permanent designs.

At the same time, the couple may want a smaller amount of lifelong coverage for final expenses or legacy goals. Permanent coverage may be reviewed for that role. The permanent policy is not trying to do the same job as the term policy. It is solving a different problem.

Now consider a person in their sixties with no mortgage and grown children. The temporary income need may be smaller, but final expense, spouse protection, legacy, business succession, or estate coordination may matter more. The mix changes because the life stage changes.

This is why the review should begin with timeline. How long does the need last? What happens when the term period ends? What premium can be maintained? Are conversion options available? Would lifelong coverage still be wanted after the temporary need is gone?

Reflection for Your Notes

As you think about the difference between term and permanent life insurance, write down what feels settled and what still feels unclear. A protection review is not about proving that you already know the answer. It is about bringing the right questions into the room so the next step is based on your life, your people, your budget, and your priorities.

Chapter 4: Final Expense and End-of-Life Cost Planning

Why Families Pause Here

Final expense planning is tender because it asks families to talk about a day nobody wants to rush toward. Done well, it is not morbid. It is a way to leave instructions, reduce confusion, and make immediate costs easier for the people who are grieving.

In a healthy planning conversation, reducing confusion at a difficult time is the starting point. The goal is not to make anyone anxious or to make a product sound perfect. The goal is to understand what the coverage is supposed to protect, how long that need may last, and what tradeoffs are reasonable for the household.

Protection planning is not about fear. It is about giving the people you love more room to breathe if income, health, debt, business responsibilities, or family needs change unexpectedly.

A policy may be part of the answer, but the policy should follow the purpose. Clear goals make the product conversation calmer, more useful, and easier to review over time.

What It Means

At its simplest, final expense and end-of-life cost planning is about giving survivors direction and immediate resources. That does not mean every solution is simple. It means the purpose can be stated in ordinary language before the details begin.

Life insurance products are contracts, so premiums, underwriting, riders, exclusions, limitations, state availability, and policy terms all matter. The details should support the family goal instead of overwhelming it.

Some coverage is designed to last for a specific period. Some coverage is designed to last longer if premiums are paid and the policy stays in force. Some policies may build cash value. Some

may include riders that can help during qualifying illness events. Some products are built for protection only, while others may cross into retirement income, safe money, or legacy conversations.

Robert's adult children know he has some savings, but nobody knows what he intended for funeral costs or immediate bills.

A Simple Example

In an early conversation, it is normal not to know which type of coverage belongs in the discussion. The review should begin with the need, then narrow the options from there.

The better question is not simply what can be purchased today. The better question is what problem the coverage is supposed to solve and how the family would actually use it later.

One common misunderstanding is that final expense planning is only about a funeral. This belief can cause people to either delay planning or overcorrect with a decision that does not fit.

Common Assumptions

Another misunderstanding is that final expense and end-of-life cost planning can be judged by one feature alone. People may focus only on premium, only on cash value, only on the death benefit, only on a rider, or only on a story they heard from someone else. Those details matter, but they need context.

Another common mistake is assuming the planning is finished once a policy is placed. Life changes, employer benefits change, beneficiaries become outdated, and some policies need attention to stay aligned with the original goal.

What people often overlook with final expense and end-of-life cost planning is the family conversation around it. Someone may need to know where documents are kept, who to call, what the intended purpose is, and whether there are special family dynamics to consider.

What People Forget to Ask

Ownership and beneficiary choices deserve careful attention. The policy owner controls the contract, the insured is the person covered, and the beneficiary receives the death benefit if the policy pays.

Timing also matters. Waiting can affect insurability, premium, and available options, while moving too quickly can create regret if the policy does not match the goal.

A protection review usually looks at burial preferences, immediate cash needs, beneficiary access, existing coverage, debt, and family communication. It may also compare existing coverage with current goals and identify gaps that are not obvious from policy pages alone.

What the Review May Explore

A review may include income replacement, final expenses, mortgage protection, children, aging parents, business obligations, retirement timing, health considerations, and beneficiary updates.

The review should also ask what you do not want. Some people want temporary low-cost coverage, some want lifelong protection, some want to explore cash value carefully, and some want to avoid complexity.

If this sounds like your situation, mark the section and bring your questions to a protection review.

A Practical Summary

The main lesson of this chapter is that final expense and end-of-life cost planning should be discussed with patience and context. A policy is only useful when it supports the real-life purpose behind it.

There is no single answer that fits every family. The right conversation considers need, time horizon, budget, health, product design, and future review.

As you continue, keep asking one simple question: what would this coverage help my family preserve, avoid, or complete?

Continue With This in Mind

The next chapter turns to mortgage protection and family stability, continuing the same theme: protection planning works best when the product discussion follows the human need.

Beyond the Funeral Home

Final expense planning may include burial or cremation costs, but survivors often face other immediate expenses too. There may be travel, medical bills, utilities, small debts, probate-related delays, or simply the need for time away from work. A modest policy can be meaningful when it gives loved ones immediate direction.

The review should ask whether family members know the client's preferences, who should be contacted, and whether the beneficiary can access funds without unnecessary confusion.

The Gift of Clear Instructions

Final expense planning often works best when the policy conversation is paired with simple family communication. A person may not want to discuss every detail of end-of-life planning, but they can still make practical choices easier. They can tell a trusted person where the policy is kept, who the beneficiary is, whether arrangements have been prepaid, and what preferences matter.

The emotional value of this clarity is easy to underestimate. Families often make decisions while tired, grieving, and surrounded by unfamiliar paperwork. If they do not know what the person wanted, every choice can feel heavier. A modest policy and a few written notes can reduce the number of urgent decisions.

A review should also ask how quickly funds may be needed. Some costs arrive before a death claim is processed. Some families have savings available; others do not. The beneficiary structure matters because naming the wrong person, no person, or an estate without understanding the consequences may create delay or confusion. Legal questions should be directed to qualified counsel, but insurance beneficiary basics should still be reviewed.

Reflection for Your Notes

As you think about final expense and end-of-life cost planning, write down what feels settled and what still feels unclear. A protection review is not about proving that you already know the answer. It is about bringing the right questions into the room so the next step is based on your life, your people, your budget, and your priorities.

Chapter 5: Mortgage Protection and Family Stability

Why This Matters Now

A home is more than a loan balance. It is the place where children sleep, meals are shared, routines are built, and memories gather. Mortgage protection belongs in the conversation because the family may need options if one income is no longer there.

In a healthy planning conversation, keeping home choices open is the starting point. The goal is not to make anyone anxious or to make a product sound perfect. The goal is to understand what the coverage is supposed to protect, how long that need may last, and what tradeoffs are reasonable for the household.

Protection planning is not about fear. It is about giving the people you love more room to breathe if income, health, debt, business responsibilities, or family needs change unexpectedly.

A policy may be part of the answer, but the policy should follow the purpose. Clear goals make the product conversation calmer, more useful, and easier to review over time.

The Simple Explanation

At its simplest, mortgage protection and family stability is about protecting the place where family life happens. That does not mean every solution is simple. It means the purpose can be stated in ordinary language before the details begin.

Life insurance products are contracts, so premiums, underwriting, riders, exclusions, limitations, state availability, and policy terms all matter. The details should support the family goal instead of overwhelming it.

Some coverage is designed to last for a specific period. Some coverage is designed to last longer if premiums are paid and the policy stays in force. Some policies may build cash value. Some may include riders that can help during qualifying illness events.

Some products are built for protection only, while others may cross into retirement income, safe money, or legacy conversations.

After buying their first home, Tasha and Eli realize the mortgage payment depends on both incomes, but their workplace benefits would not cover many years of payments.

A Client-Style Scenario

In an early conversation, it is normal not to know which type of coverage belongs in the discussion. The review should begin with the need, then narrow the options from there.

The better question is not simply what can be purchased today. The better question is what problem the coverage is supposed to solve and how the family would actually use it later.

One common misunderstanding is that the lender's offer is the same as a family protection plan. This belief can cause people to either delay planning or overcorrect with a decision that does not fit.

What Gets Misunderstood

Another misunderstanding is that mortgage protection and family stability can be judged by one feature alone. People may focus only on premium, only on cash value, only on the death benefit, only on a rider, or only on a story they heard from someone else. Those details matter, but they need context.

Another common mistake is assuming the planning is finished once a policy is placed. Life changes, employer benefits change, beneficiaries become outdated, and some policies need attention to stay aligned with the original goal.

What people often overlook with mortgage protection and family stability is the family conversation around it. Someone may need to know where documents are kept, who to call, what the intended purpose is, and whether there are special family dynamics to consider.

What Often Gets Missed

Ownership and beneficiary choices deserve careful attention. The policy owner controls the contract, the insured is the person covered, and the beneficiary receives the death benefit if the policy pays.

Timing also matters. Waiting can affect insurability, premium, and available options, while moving too quickly can create regret if the policy does not match the goal.

A protection review usually looks at mortgage balance, income replacement, survivor options, ownership, portability, and affordability. It may also compare existing coverage with current goals and identify gaps that are not obvious from policy pages alone.

Inside a Thoughtful Review

A review may include income replacement, final expenses, mortgage protection, children, aging parents, business obligations, retirement timing, health considerations, and beneficiary updates.

The review should also ask what you do not want. Some people want temporary low-cost coverage, some want lifelong protection, some want to explore cash value carefully, and some want to avoid complexity.

If this sounds like your situation, mark the section and bring your questions to a protection review.

Chapter Summary

The main lesson of this chapter is that mortgage protection and family stability should be discussed with patience and context. A policy is only useful when it supports the real-life purpose behind it.

There is no single answer that fits every family. The right conversation considers need, time horizon, budget, health, product design, and future review.

As you continue, keep asking one simple question: what would this coverage help my family preserve, avoid, or complete?

Next Conversation

The next chapter turns to whole life insurance explained simply, continuing the same theme: protection planning works best when the product discussion follows the human need.

The Home Decision

Mortgage protection is not only about paying off a house. It is about giving survivors choices. One family may want to pay the mortgage completely. Another may only need enough income support to keep payments current while deciding whether to stay, sell, refinance, or move closer to family.

That difference matters. A review can compare the mortgage balance, survivor income, other debts, savings, children's needs, and whether coverage should be tied to the loan or owned personally by the family.

Staying Is Not the Only Goal

Mortgage protection conversations should be careful because families do not all want the same outcome. Some survivors want to remain in the home no matter what. Others may want time to decide. A spouse may want to stay until the children finish school, then downsize. A family may want enough cash to sell the home on their own terms rather than under pressure.

That is why mortgage protection is not only about matching a policy amount to a loan balance. A review may look at the mortgage, but it should also look at income, savings, child care, taxes, maintenance, insurance, and whether the surviving family member could comfortably manage the home.

Ownership and portability matter too. Some coverage offered around a mortgage may be tied to the lender or loan. Individually owned life insurance may offer different control and beneficiary options, depending on underwriting and product design. The review should explain those differences without assuming one path is automatically best.

Reflection for Your Notes

As you think about mortgage protection and family stability, write down what feels settled and what still feels unclear. A protection review is not about proving that you already know the answer. It is about bringing the right questions into the room so the next step is based on your life, your people, your budget, and your priorities.

Chapter 6: Whole Life Insurance Explained Simply

The Real-Life Reason

Whole life insurance can be misunderstood because people often hear the strongest opinions first. Some hear that it is always too expensive. Others hear that it is a perfect financial tool. The truth is quieter: it can be useful when its guarantees, costs, cash value, and long-term purpose fit the client.

In a healthy planning conversation, permanent protection with guarantees and tradeoffs is the starting point. The goal is not to make anyone anxious or to make a product sound perfect. The goal is to understand what the coverage is supposed to protect, how long that need may last, and what tradeoffs are reasonable for the household.

Protection planning is not about fear. It is about giving the people you love more room to breathe if income, health, debt, business responsibilities, or family needs change unexpectedly.

A policy may be part of the answer, but the policy should follow the purpose. Clear goals make the product conversation calmer, more useful, and easier to review over time.

Plain English First

At its simplest, whole life insurance explained simply is about providing lifelong death benefit protection when it fits the goals and budget. That does not mean every solution is simple. It means the purpose can be stated in ordinary language before the details begin.

Life insurance products are contracts, so premiums, underwriting, riders, exclusions, limitations, state availability, and policy terms all matter. The details should support the family goal instead of overwhelming it.

Some coverage is designed to last for a specific period. Some coverage is designed to last longer if premiums are paid and the

policy stays in force. Some policies may build cash value. Some may include riders that can help during qualifying illness events. Some products are built for protection only, while others may cross into retirement income, safe money, or legacy conversations.

Janice wants a predictable policy she can keep beyond retirement, but she also needs to understand premiums, guarantees, and access limits.

How This Can Show Up

In an early conversation, it is normal not to know which type of coverage belongs in the discussion. The review should begin with the need, then narrow the options from there.

The better question is not simply what can be purchased today. The better question is what problem the coverage is supposed to solve and how the family would actually use it later.

One common misunderstanding is that whole life is either magic or always too expensive. This belief can cause people to either delay planning or overcorrect with a decision that does not fit.

A Common Misread

Another misunderstanding is that whole life insurance explained simply can be judged by one feature alone. People may focus only on premium, only on cash value, only on the death benefit, only on a rider, or only on a story they heard from someone else. Those details matter, but they need context.

Another common mistake is assuming the planning is finished once a policy is placed. Life changes, employer benefits change, beneficiaries become outdated, and some policies need attention to stay aligned with the original goal.

What people often overlook with whole life insurance explained simply is the family conversation around it. Someone may need to know where documents are kept, who to call, what the intended purpose is, and whether there are special family dynamics to consider.

The Quiet Details

Ownership and beneficiary choices deserve careful attention. The policy owner controls the contract, the insured is the person covered, and the beneficiary receives the death benefit if the policy pays.

Timing also matters. Waiting can affect insurability, premium, and available options, while moving too quickly can create regret if the policy does not match the goal.

A protection review usually looks at premium commitment, guarantees, dividend assumptions if applicable, cash value access, beneficiary goals, and suitability. It may also compare existing coverage with current goals and identify gaps that are not obvious from policy pages alone.

What an Advisor Looks For

A review may include income replacement, final expenses, mortgage protection, children, aging parents, business obligations, retirement timing, health considerations, and beneficiary updates.

The review should also ask what you do not want. Some people want temporary low-cost coverage, some want lifelong protection, some want to explore cash value carefully, and some want to avoid complexity.

If this sounds like your situation, mark the section and bring your questions to a protection review.

In Short

The main lesson of this chapter is that whole life insurance explained simply should be discussed with patience and context. A policy is only useful when it supports the real-life purpose behind it.

There is no single answer that fits every family. The right conversation considers need, time horizon, budget, health, product design, and future review.

As you continue, keep asking one simple question: what would this coverage help my family preserve, avoid, or complete?

A Soft Step Forward

The next chapter turns to children's whole life insurance: when it may make sense, continuing the same theme: protection planning works best when the product discussion follows the human need.

Where Whole Life Can Fit

Whole life insurance is often discussed as permanent coverage with level premiums, guaranteed cash value growth according to the contract, and a death benefit designed to last for life if the policy is properly maintained. Those guarantees can appeal to people who want predictability. They can also come with higher premiums than term insurance for the same initial death benefit.

That tradeoff is the heart of the conversation. Whole life may make sense when the client wants lifelong protection, final expense funding, a legacy amount, conservative cash value accumulation, or a policy that is not tied to a temporary term period. It may not make sense if the premium would crowd out emergency savings, retirement contributions, debt reduction, or needed term coverage for a larger temporary risk.

Some policies may pay dividends, but dividends are not guaranteed unless specifically stated by the issuing carrier. A review should separate guaranteed values from non-guaranteed assumptions so the client understands what is promised and what is only projected.

What to Ask Before Buying or Keeping It

Before starting or replacing a whole life policy, ask what role it plays in the total plan. Is it meant for final expenses, family legacy, business planning, cash value access, or lifelong coverage? How long are premiums payable? What happens if you need to reduce coverage? Are there surrender charges or loan interest? Does the policy still fit if income changes? These are not objections. They are healthy planning questions.

Keeping Expectations Grounded

Whole life should be reviewed with both appreciation and caution. The guarantees can be valuable, but the premium must fit. Cash value can be useful, but it takes time. A death benefit can support legacy planning, but it should be coordinated with beneficiary choices and other family resources.

The Commitment Side of Whole Life

Whole life is not only a purchase; it is a commitment. The premium pattern, guarantees, cash value schedule, loan provisions, and death benefit should be understood before the policy is started. A client should know whether the policy is designed for lifetime payments, limited payments, or another structure. They should know what happens if they stop paying, reduce coverage, borrow, or surrender.

For some clients, that commitment is exactly why whole life feels appealing. They like the discipline, the guaranteed values, and the idea of coverage that does not expire after a term period. For others, the same commitment may be too heavy. A policy that cannot be comfortably maintained is not a strong fit, even if the concept sounds attractive.

A careful review also compares whole life with the rest of the household plan. Does the family have emergency savings? Are high-interest debts under control? Is temporary income protection adequate? Are retirement contributions or care planning being ignored? Whole life can be a valuable piece, but it should not crowd out the foundation.

When Keeping an Older Whole Life Policy Deserves Care

Many clients already own a whole life policy purchased years ago by a parent, grandparent, employer program, or previous advisor. Before surrendering, replacing, borrowing from, or ignoring that policy, it deserves a careful review. Older policies may have guarantees, dividend histories, cash values, loan provisions, or premium structures that should be understood before any change is made.

A review may look at the current death benefit, cash surrender value, outstanding loans, annual premium, dividend option, beneficiary, and projected values. It may also ask whether the policy still solves a real need. Sometimes an older whole life policy is worth keeping because it provides stable lifelong coverage. Sometimes it needs attention because loans are building, premiums are uncomfortable, or the beneficiary is outdated.

The key is not to make an emotional decision based on one number. The key is to understand what the policy is doing now, what it may do later, and how any change could affect protection, taxes, and family goals.

Reflection for Your Notes

As you think about whole life insurance explained simply, write down what feels settled and what still feels unclear. A protection review is not about proving that you already know the answer. It is about bringing the right questions into the room so the next step is based on your life, your people, your budget, and your priorities.

Chapter 7: Children's Whole Life Insurance: When It May Make Sense

Start With the Human Need

Coverage on a child should be handled with extra care because the emotional pull is real. Parents and grandparents naturally want to do something protective and lasting, but the first question should be whether the adults in the household are already properly protected.

In a healthy planning conversation, protecting future insurability carefully is the starting point. The goal is not to make anyone anxious or to make a product sound perfect. The goal is to understand what the coverage is supposed to protect, how long that need may last, and what tradeoffs are reasonable for the household.

Protection planning is not about fear. It is about giving the people you love more room to breathe if income, health, debt, business responsibilities, or family needs change unexpectedly.

A policy may be part of the answer, but the policy should follow the purpose. Clear goals make the product conversation calmer, more useful, and easier to review over time.

How the Concept Works

At its simplest, children's whole life insurance: when it may make sense is about considering a small lifelong policy as part of a balanced legacy conversation. That does not mean every solution is simple. It means the purpose can be stated in ordinary language before the details begin.

Life insurance products are contracts, so premiums, underwriting, riders, exclusions, limitations, state availability, and policy terms all matter. The details should support the family goal instead of overwhelming it.

Some coverage is designed to last for a specific period. Some coverage is designed to last longer if premiums are paid and the policy stays in force. Some policies may build cash value. Some may include riders that can help during qualifying illness events. Some products are built for protection only, while others may cross into retirement income, safe money, or legacy conversations.

Grandparents want to do something meaningful for their new grandchild and ask whether a small permanent policy could be a lasting gift.

Important Nuance

Children's whole life insurance should be discussed carefully. Potential benefits may include protection of future insurability, a small lifelong death benefit, early cash value education, and a meaningful gifting or legacy conversation. Those benefits do not make it right for every household.

Adult protection usually comes first. If parents or guardians are underinsured, putting money toward a child's policy while leaving the household exposed may not be the strongest order of priorities. A review can help decide whether a child policy is affordable after core family protection is addressed.

Ownership and long-term responsibility matter. Someone must pay premiums, understand the policy, and eventually decide whether and how the child should take over ownership. The policy should be explained as a financial tool with limits, not as a guaranteed solution to every future need.

A Familiar Situation

In an early conversation, it is normal not to know which type of coverage belongs in the discussion. The review should begin with the need, then narrow the options from there.

The better question is not simply what can be purchased today. The better question is what problem the coverage is supposed to solve and how the family would actually use it later.

One common misunderstanding is that buying coverage for a child should replace adult protection. This belief can cause people to either delay planning or overcorrect with a decision that does not fit.

Where Confusion Begins

Another misunderstanding is that children's whole life insurance: when it may make sense can be judged by one feature alone. People may focus only on premium, only on cash value, only on the death benefit, only on a rider, or only on a story they heard from someone else. Those details matter, but they need context.

Another common mistake is assuming the planning is finished once a policy is placed. Life changes, employer benefits change, beneficiaries become outdated, and some policies need attention to stay aligned with the original goal.

What people often overlook with children's whole life insurance: when it may make sense is the family conversation around it. Someone may need to know where documents are kept, who to call, what the intended purpose is, and whether there are special family dynamics to consider.

The Overlooked Pieces

Ownership and beneficiary choices deserve careful attention. The policy owner controls the contract, the insured is the person covered, and the beneficiary receives the death benefit if the policy pays.

Timing also matters. Waiting can affect insurability, premium, and available options, while moving too quickly can create regret if the policy does not match the goal.

A protection review usually looks at family budget, parent coverage, child insurability, ownership, cash value education, gifting intent, and long-term responsibility. It may also compare existing coverage with current goals and identify gaps that are not obvious from policy pages alone.

Review Questions to Bring Forward

A review may include income replacement, final expenses, mortgage protection, children, aging parents, business obligations, retirement timing, health considerations, and beneficiary updates.

The review should also ask what you do not want. Some people want temporary low-cost coverage, some want lifelong protection, some want to explore cash value carefully, and some want to avoid complexity.

If this sounds like your situation, mark the section and bring your questions to a protection review.

The Main Point

The main lesson of this chapter is that children's whole life insurance: when it may make sense should be discussed with patience and context. A policy is only useful when it supports the real-life purpose behind it.

There is no single answer that fits every family. The right conversation considers need, time horizon, budget, health, product design, and future review.

As you continue, keep asking one simple question: what would this coverage help my family preserve, avoid, or complete?

Looking Ahead

The next chapter turns to universal life and indexed universal life education, continuing the same theme: protection planning works best when the product discussion follows the human need.

A Balanced Family Conversation

Children's whole life insurance can be a loving gift, but it should not be treated as an automatic first step. In many households, the strongest protection move is to make sure the parents or guardians have enough coverage first. If the adults' income, caregiving, or debt responsibilities are not protected, the family may still be exposed even if a child owns a small policy.

When it fits, a child's policy may protect future insurability in a limited way, create a small permanent death benefit, and introduce the child to the idea that financial tools require care. Grandparents may see it as a legacy gift. Parents may see it as a way to start something early while premiums are manageable. Those can be valid reasons when the budget allows and expectations are realistic.

The limitations should be just as clear. The death benefit may be modest. Cash value usually takes time to build. The policy may need premiums for many years. Ownership should be handled carefully, especially when the child becomes an adult. It should not be sold as a substitute for college savings, adult coverage, emergency savings, or a complete family plan.

Review Questions for Parents and Grandparents

Before moving forward, ask whether the adults are adequately insured, who will own the policy, who will pay premiums, what happens if the payer dies or becomes unable to continue, and when the child should learn about the policy. Also ask whether the same premium could solve a more urgent family need. A good answer respects both the heart behind the gift and the household's practical priorities.

Teaching the Policy Later

One overlooked part of children's whole life is the future conversation with the child. If a parent or grandparent starts a policy when the child is young, someone eventually needs to explain what it is, why it was purchased, who owns it, and what responsibilities come with it. Without that conversation, the policy can become another forgotten document.

Handled well, the policy can become a teaching tool. It can introduce the child, later as a teenager or adult, to ideas such as premiums, beneficiaries, cash value, loans, guarantees, and long-term planning. The lesson should be balanced. The child should understand that insurance is not magic and that cash value is not a toy. They should also understand the generosity behind the gift.

A review can help parents and grandparents decide whether the gift is practical. If the family is choosing between paying for a child policy and protecting the income of the parent who supports the household, adult coverage may deserve priority. If core protection is already addressed and the premium is manageable, a small child policy may have a place.

Grandparent Gifts and Family Coordination

Grandparents often ask about children's whole life because they want to give something more lasting than toys or cash. That intention is generous, and it deserves a thoughtful structure. The review should ask whether the parents know about the policy, who will own it, who will receive statements, and how premium payments will continue if the grandparent can no longer pay.

Family coordination helps prevent confusion later. A parent may need to know that a policy exists so it is not lost. The family may need to decide whether ownership should transfer when the child becomes an adult. If multiple grandchildren are involved, grandparents may want to think about fairness, affordability, and whether every policy should be designed the same way.

This conversation can be warm without being unrealistic. A child policy may be a meaningful legacy gift, but it should be coordinated with the family's larger financial picture. The gift should strengthen the family, not create hidden obligations or misunderstandings.

Reflection for Your Notes

As you think about children's whole life insurance: when it may make sense, write down what feels settled and what still feels unclear. A protection review is not about proving that you already know the answer. It is about bringing the right questions into the room so the next step is based on your life, your people, your budget, and your priorities.

Chapter 8: Universal Life and Indexed Universal Life Education

Why Families Pause Here

Universal life and indexed universal life are easier to discuss when the word flexible is treated with respect. Flexibility can be helpful, but it also means there are moving parts that should be monitored, explained, and reviewed over time.

In a healthy planning conversation, flexibility that requires attention is the starting point. The goal is not to make anyone anxious or to make a product sound perfect. The goal is to understand what the coverage is supposed to protect, how long that need may last, and what tradeoffs are reasonable for the household.

Protection planning is not about fear. It is about giving the people you love more room to breathe if income, health, debt, business responsibilities, or family needs change unexpectedly.

A policy may be part of the answer, but the policy should follow the purpose. Clear goals make the product conversation calmer, more useful, and easier to review over time.

What It Means

At its simplest, universal life and indexed universal life education is about understanding flexible permanent insurance designs before relying on them. That does not mean every solution is simple. It means the purpose can be stated in ordinary language before the details begin.

Life insurance products are contracts, so premiums, underwriting, riders, exclusions, limitations, state availability, and policy terms all matter. The details should support the family goal instead of overwhelming it.

Some coverage is designed to last for a specific period. Some coverage is designed to last longer if premiums are paid and the

policy stays in force. Some policies may build cash value. Some may include riders that can help during qualifying illness events. Some products are built for protection only, while others may cross into retirement income, safe money, or legacy conversations.

Calvin heard that indexed universal life could help with future income. A review helps him separate the concept from the actual moving parts.

Important Nuance

Universal life is known for flexibility. Premium payments, death benefit options, and policy values can vary based on the contract and how it is funded. That flexibility can be useful, but it also means the policy needs monitoring.

Indexed universal life credits interest based on a formula tied to an external index, subject to caps, floors, participation rates, spreads, or other contract terms. The policyholder is not directly invested in the index. Charges and crediting rules can change within contract limits.

Illustrations are not promises of future performance. They are educational tools based on assumptions. A responsible review asks what happens if crediting is lower, charges rise, loans are taken, or premiums are reduced.

A Simple Example

In an early conversation, it is normal not to know which type of coverage belongs in the discussion. The review should begin with the need, then narrow the options from there.

The better question is not simply what can be purchased today. The better question is what problem the coverage is supposed to solve and how the family would actually use it later.

One common misunderstanding is that index-linked interest means stock market investing without risk. This belief can cause people to either delay planning or overcorrect with a decision that does not fit.

Common Assumptions

Another misunderstanding is that universal life and indexed universal life education can be judged by one feature alone. People may focus only on premium, only on cash value, only on the death benefit, only on a rider, or only on a story they heard from someone else. Those details matter, but they need context.

Another common mistake is assuming the planning is finished once a policy is placed. Life changes, employer benefits change, beneficiaries become outdated, and some policies need attention to stay aligned with the original goal.

What people often overlook with universal life and indexed universal life education is the family conversation around it. Someone may need to know where documents are kept, who to call, what the intended purpose is, and whether there are special family dynamics to consider.

What People Forget to Ask

Ownership and beneficiary choices deserve careful attention. The policy owner controls the contract, the insured is the person covered, and the beneficiary receives the death benefit if the policy pays.

Timing also matters. Waiting can affect insurability, premium, and available options, while moving too quickly can create regret if the policy does not match the goal.

A protection review usually looks at premium funding, caps, floors, charges, illustrated values, policy monitoring, lapse risk, and whether the design matches the goal. It may also compare existing coverage with current goals and identify gaps that are not obvious from policy pages alone.

What the Review May Explore

A review may include income replacement, final expenses, mortgage protection, children, aging parents, business obligations, retirement timing, health considerations, and beneficiary updates.

The review should also ask what you do not want. Some people want temporary low-cost coverage, some want lifelong protection, some want to explore cash value carefully, and some want to avoid complexity.

If this sounds like your situation, mark the section and bring your questions to a protection review.

A Practical Summary

The main lesson of this chapter is that universal life and indexed universal life education should be discussed with patience and context. A policy is only useful when it supports the real-life purpose behind it.

There is no single answer that fits every family. The right conversation considers need, time horizon, budget, health, product design, and future review.

As you continue, keep asking one simple question: what would this coverage help my family preserve, avoid, or complete?

Continue With This in Mind

The next chapter turns to living benefits and protection while you are alive, continuing the same theme: protection planning works best when the product discussion follows the human need.

Understanding the Moving Parts

Universal life is not one single experience. Some designs emphasize flexible premiums. Some emphasize death benefit protection. Some are built with cash value accumulation in mind. Indexed universal life adds an interest-crediting method tied to an external index, but the policyholder is not directly invested in that index. The contract determines how interest is credited and how charges are assessed.

That means the illustration deserves careful reading. Caps, floors, participation rates, spreads, policy charges, cost of insurance charges, loan provisions, and premium assumptions can all affect the long-term outcome. A policy may look strong under one set of assumptions and much weaker under another. The review should ask what happens if the policy is funded below target, if index credits are lower than illustrated, if loans are taken early, or if charges increase within contract limits.

Indexed universal life can be part of an educational conversation about protection, cash value, and possible supplemental income planning, but it should not be described as market investing without consequences. It is insurance first. Suitability, funding discipline, and monitoring matter.

What Ongoing Review Looks Like

A client who owns universal life or indexed universal life should not put the policy in a drawer forever. Reviews may look at current cash value, death benefit option, premium history, projected lapse age, loan activity, current crediting assumptions, and whether the original goal still applies. Sometimes the right action is to keep funding as planned. Sometimes it is to adjust expectations. Sometimes it is to compare alternatives. The value is in knowing before there is a problem.

Stress Testing the Illustration

One of the most helpful review practices is asking for less favorable scenarios. What if premiums are skipped? What if crediting is lower? What if loans are taken? What if the policy needs to last longer than expected? A policy that only works under perfect assumptions deserves more discussion.

Why Funding Discipline Matters

Universal life policies can be sensitive to how they are funded. Paying the minimum may keep a policy active for a time but may not support the long-term goal shown in an illustration. Paying irregularly may be workable in some designs, but it can also create problems if charges continue and policy values are not strong enough.

For indexed universal life, the client should understand that index interest credits may vary. A year with strong index performance does not mean every year will look that way. A year with low crediting does not automatically mean the policy is failing. The question is whether the policy was designed and funded with enough room for real life.

This is where annual reviews are especially important. The review can compare actual performance with the original assumptions, look at current charges, evaluate loan activity, and decide whether the premium pattern still supports the intended death benefit or income conversation. Flexibility is useful only when someone is paying attention.

Reading an Illustration With Adult Eyes

An illustration can be useful, but it should never be treated like a guarantee unless the values are specifically guaranteed by the contract. Clients should ask which columns are guaranteed, which are current, and which are hypothetical. They should ask whether the premium shown is required, planned, minimum, or target. They should ask how long the policy is projected to last under different assumptions.

For indexed universal life, the review should also discuss how the index crediting method works. The index may perform well, but the policy crediting formula may limit gains through caps, participation rates, or spreads. The policy may also have a floor, but the floor does not erase policy charges. A year with no interest credit may still be a year when charges are deducted.

When clients understand this, they can evaluate the policy more calmly. They do not have to reject the concept or accept the sales story. They can ask whether the design is durable enough for their actual purpose.

When Flexibility Helps and When It Hurts

Flexibility can help a client adjust to changing income, changing goals, or changing protection needs. It can also create a false sense of ease if the client assumes flexible means effortless. A universal life policy may allow premium flexibility, but charges still need to be supported. An indexed universal life policy may have attractive illustrated values, but the policy still depends on funding, crediting, charges, and monitoring.

A careful advisor does not make flexibility sound better than it is. Instead, the advisor explains what must be watched. That includes premium patterns, policy value, loan balances, current assumptions, and the projected ability of the policy to stay in force. A flexible policy can be useful when the owner understands the responsibility that comes with it.

Reflection for Your Notes

As you think about universal life and indexed universal life education, write down what feels settled and what still feels unclear. A protection review is not about proving that you already know the answer. It is about bringing the right questions into the room so the next step is based on your life, your people, your budget, and your priorities.

Chapter 9: Living Benefits and Protection While You Are Alive

Why This Matters Now

Some of the hardest financial seasons happen while a person is still living. A serious diagnosis, chronic illness, or qualifying medical event can affect income, caregiving, travel, savings, and family routines long before a death benefit would ever be paid.

In a healthy planning conversation, coverage that may help during qualifying illness is the starting point. The goal is not to make anyone anxious or to make a product sound perfect. The goal is to understand what the coverage is supposed to protect, how long that need may last, and what tradeoffs are reasonable for the household.

Protection planning is not about fear. It is about giving the people you love more room to breathe if income, health, debt, business responsibilities, or family needs change unexpectedly.

A policy may be part of the answer, but the policy should follow the purpose. Clear goals make the product conversation calmer, more useful, and easier to review over time.

The Simple Explanation

At its simplest, living benefits and protection while you are alive is about planning for life events that happen before death. That does not mean every solution is simple. It means the purpose can be stated in ordinary language before the details begin.

Life insurance products are contracts, so premiums, underwriting, riders, exclusions, limitations, state availability, and policy terms all matter. The details should support the family goal instead of overwhelming it.

Some coverage is designed to last for a specific period. Some coverage is designed to last longer if premiums are paid and the policy stays in force. Some policies may build cash value. Some

may include riders that can help during qualifying illness events. Some products are built for protection only, while others may cross into retirement income, safe money, or legacy conversations.

Maya's family has seen how a diagnosis can affect income, travel, caregiving, and savings before death ever occurs.

A Client-Style Scenario

In an early conversation, it is normal not to know which type of coverage belongs in the discussion. The review should begin with the need, then narrow the options from there.

The better question is not simply what can be purchased today. The better question is what problem the coverage is supposed to solve and how the family would actually use it later.

One common misunderstanding is that living benefits are the same as health insurance or long-term care insurance. This belief can cause people to either delay planning or overcorrect with a decision that does not fit.

What Gets Misunderstood

Another misunderstanding is that living benefits and protection while you are alive can be judged by one feature alone. People may focus only on premium, only on cash value, only on the death benefit, only on a rider, or only on a story they heard from someone else. Those details matter, but they need context.

Another common mistake is assuming the planning is finished once a policy is placed. Life changes, employer benefits change, beneficiaries become outdated, and some policies need attention to stay aligned with the original goal.

What people often overlook with living benefits and protection while you are alive is the family conversation around it. Someone may need to know where documents are kept, who to call, what the intended purpose is, and whether there are special family dynamics to consider.

What Often Gets Missed

Ownership and beneficiary choices deserve careful attention. The policy owner controls the contract, the insured is the person covered, and the beneficiary receives the death benefit if the policy pays.

Timing also matters. Waiting can affect insurability, premium, and available options, while moving too quickly can create regret if the policy does not match the goal.

A protection review usually looks at rider definitions, triggers, costs, reductions, exclusions, medical underwriting, and coordination with other plans. It may also compare existing coverage with current goals and identify gaps that are not obvious from policy pages alone.

Inside a Thoughtful Review

A review may include income replacement, final expenses, mortgage protection, children, aging parents, business obligations, retirement timing, health considerations, and beneficiary updates.

The review should also ask what you do not want. Some people want temporary low-cost coverage, some want lifelong protection, some want to explore cash value carefully, and some want to avoid complexity.

If this sounds like your situation, mark the section and bring your questions to a protection review.

Chapter Summary

The main lesson of this chapter is that living benefits and protection while you are alive should be discussed with patience and context. A policy is only useful when it supports the real-life purpose behind it.

There is no single answer that fits every family. The right conversation considers need, time horizon, budget, health, product design, and future review.

As you continue, keep asking one simple question: what would this coverage help my family preserve, avoid, or complete?

Next Conversation

The next chapter turns to cash value, policy loans, and important tradeoffs, continuing the same theme: protection planning works best when the product discussion follows the human need.

Why Living Benefits Matter

Living benefits can change how a family thinks about protection. Traditional life insurance focuses on money paid after death. Certain riders may allow access to a portion of the death benefit during life if the insured meets specific qualifying conditions, such as terminal illness, chronic illness, or critical illness, depending on the policy.

The definitions matter. A chronic illness rider may require an inability to perform certain activities of daily living or substantial cognitive impairment. A critical illness rider may list specific covered conditions. A terminal illness rider may require a life expectancy certification. The exact triggers, waiting periods, fees, administrative requirements, and benefit reductions vary by carrier and product.

Living benefits are not the same as health insurance, disability insurance, or a full long-term care plan. They may help, but they may also reduce the death benefit available to beneficiaries. That is why the conversation should include both the living need and the survivor need.

A Family-Centered Example

Imagine a spouse who survives a heart attack but cannot return to work quickly. The family may need money for travel to specialists, home adjustments, temporary help, or replacing income. A living benefit rider, if available and if the event qualifies, may provide some financial flexibility. But the family still needs to understand how using that benefit affects the policy later. A review with Kayla can help clients look at these questions before a crisis forces rushed decisions.

Coordinating With Other Coverage

Living benefits should be discussed alongside other protections, not in isolation. A family may also have health insurance, disability coverage, emergency savings, long-term care coverage, workplace benefits, or retirement assets. Each resource has a different purpose. Health insurance helps with covered medical costs. Disability insurance may replace income. Long-term care planning may address extended care needs. Living benefit riders may provide access to life insurance benefits under specific conditions.

The overlap can be helpful, but it can also create confusion. A client may assume a chronic illness rider pays for all care needs. Another may assume a critical illness rider covers every serious condition. The review should read definitions carefully and explain what must happen before benefits may be available.

Families should also understand the tradeoff. Using a living benefit may reduce the death benefit available later. That may be acceptable if the living need is urgent, but it should be understood before the claim. The point of education is to make the choice less surprising.

The Claim Moment

It is one thing to own a policy with living benefits. It is another thing to understand what happens when someone tries to use them. A claim may require medical records, physician statements, diagnosis details, proof that policy definitions are met, and time for carrier review. The family should know that benefit access is not automatic just because an illness feels serious.

This does not make living benefits unimportant. It makes education important. Clients should know where the policy is, what riders are included, who to call, and what broad conditions may qualify. They should also understand that accessing benefits may reduce what beneficiaries receive later.

A review before illness can make the claim moment less confusing. It can identify whether living benefits exist, whether dedicated long-term care or disability planning should also be discussed, and whether the family has enough liquidity for costs that may arise before any rider benefit is approved.

Reflection for Your Notes

As you think about living benefits and protection while you are alive, write down what feels settled and what still feels unclear. A protection review is not about proving that you already know the answer. It is about bringing the right questions into the room so the next step is based on your life, your people, your budget, and your priorities.

Chapter 10: Cash Value, Policy Loans, and Important Tradeoffs

The Real-Life Reason

Cash value conversations should be slow and plainspoken. Access to policy value can be helpful in the right design, but loans, withdrawals, charges, interest, tax consequences, and lapse risk are not fine print details. They are part of the real planning conversation.

In a healthy planning conversation, understanding access before relying on it is the starting point. The goal is not to make anyone anxious or to make a product sound perfect. The goal is to understand what the coverage is supposed to protect, how long that need may last, and what tradeoffs are reasonable for the household.

Protection planning is not about fear. It is about giving the people you love more room to breathe if income, health, debt, business responsibilities, or family needs change unexpectedly.

A policy may be part of the answer, but the policy should follow the purpose. Clear goals make the product conversation calmer, more useful, and easier to review over time.

Plain English First

At its simplest, cash value, policy loans, and important tradeoffs is about learning how policy values can help and how they can create risk. That does not mean every solution is simple. It means the purpose can be stated in ordinary language before the details begin.

Life insurance products are contracts, so premiums, underwriting, riders, exclusions, limitations, state availability, and policy terms all matter. The details should support the family goal instead of overwhelming it.

Some coverage is designed to last for a specific period. Some coverage is designed to last longer if premiums are paid and the policy stays in force. Some policies may build cash value. Some may include riders that can help during qualifying illness events. Some products are built for protection only, while others may cross into retirement income, safe money, or legacy conversations.

A business owner likes the idea of accessible cash value, then learns how loan interest, policy performance, and lapse risk can affect the outcome.

Important Nuance

Cash value may be accessible through withdrawals or policy loans, depending on the product and contract terms. Access is not the same as a bank account. Loans can accrue interest. Withdrawals can reduce cash value and death benefit. Improperly managed access can contribute to lapse risk.

Cash value strategies, including personal banking or infinite banking concepts, should be presented as educational concepts only. They require careful policy design, disciplined funding, realistic assumptions, and ongoing review. They are not appropriate for everyone.

A policy can fail to meet expectations if it is underfunded, over-loaned, surrendered at the wrong time, or treated as risk-free. The tradeoffs should be understood before the policy becomes part of a larger financial strategy.

How This Can Show Up

In an early conversation, it is normal not to know which type of coverage belongs in the discussion. The review should begin with the need, then narrow the options from there.

The better question is not simply what can be purchased today. The better question is what problem the coverage is supposed to solve and how the family would actually use it later.

One common misunderstanding is that policy loans never have consequences. This belief can cause people to either delay planning or overcorrect with a decision that does not fit.

A Common Misread

Another misunderstanding is that cash value, policy loans, and important tradeoffs can be judged by one feature alone. People may focus only on premium, only on cash value, only on the death benefit, only on a rider, or only on a story they heard from someone else. Those details matter, but they need context.

Another common mistake is assuming the planning is finished once a policy is placed. Life changes, employer benefits change, beneficiaries become outdated, and some policies need attention to stay aligned with the original goal.

What people often overlook with cash value, policy loans, and important tradeoffs is the family conversation around it. Someone may need to know where documents are kept, who to call, what the intended purpose is, and whether there are special family dynamics to consider.

The Quiet Details

Ownership and beneficiary choices deserve careful attention. The policy owner controls the contract, the insured is the person covered, and the beneficiary receives the death benefit if the policy pays.

Timing also matters. Waiting can affect insurability, premium, and available options, while moving too quickly can create regret if the policy does not match the goal.

A protection review usually looks at fees, surrender charges, loan rates, tax considerations, death benefit reductions, and stress testing. It may also compare existing coverage with current goals and identify gaps that are not obvious from policy pages alone.

What an Advisor Looks For

A review may include income replacement, final expenses, mortgage protection, children, aging parents, business obligations, retirement timing, health considerations, and beneficiary updates.

The review should also ask what you do not want. Some people want temporary low-cost coverage, some want lifelong protection, some want to explore cash value carefully, and some want to avoid complexity.

If this sounds like your situation, mark the section and bring your questions to a protection review.

In Short

The main lesson of this chapter is that cash value, policy loans, and important tradeoffs should be discussed with patience and context. A policy is only useful when it supports the real-life purpose behind it.

There is no single answer that fits every family. The right conversation considers need, time horizon, budget, health, product design, and future review.

As you continue, keep asking one simple question: what would this coverage help my family preserve, avoid, or complete?

A Soft Step Forward

The next chapter turns to life insurance for retirement and safe money conversations, continuing the same theme: protection planning works best when the product discussion follows the human need.

Cash Value Is a Tool, Not a Shortcut

Cash value can be useful because it may give a policy owner access to value during life. That access can support flexibility, emergencies, business opportunities, education planning, retirement conversations, or other goals. But it should never be explained as free money. The policy owner is using value inside an insurance contract, and the contract rules matter.

Withdrawals can reduce cash value and death benefit. Policy loans can accrue interest. If loan balances grow too large, the policy may lapse and create tax consequences. Surrendering a policy may trigger charges or taxable gain. Underfunding a policy designed for cash value can weaken the entire strategy.

Personal banking or infinite banking concepts should be discussed only as educational concepts requiring careful review. They depend on policy design, funding discipline, loan behavior, and long-term monitoring. They are not appropriate for every family, and they should not distract from basic protection needs.

Questions Before Using Cash Value

Before borrowing or withdrawing, ask why the money is needed, whether there are other sources of liquidity, how the transaction affects the death benefit, what interest rate applies, whether the policy could lapse, and how repayment will be handled. A review should also look at the original purpose of the policy. If the death benefit is needed for a spouse, child, business partner, or estate goal, access decisions should be made carefully.

Before a Loan Becomes a Habit

Policy loans can feel easy because they may not require the same approval process as a bank loan. That convenience can be risky if the owner forgets that interest accrues and the death benefit may be reduced. A review can help decide whether a loan supports the plan or slowly weakens it.

The Lapse Risk Nobody Wants to Meet Late

Policy lapse risk deserves plain language. If loans and interest grow, if premiums are not paid, or if policy values are not enough to support charges, a policy may lapse. When a policy with gain lapses after loans have been taken, there may be tax consequences.

That possibility surprises many people because they thought borrowing from a policy was always simple.

This does not mean policy loans are bad. It means they should be managed. A client may borrow for a business need, emergency, education cost, or retirement income strategy. The review should ask how the loan will be repaid, whether interest will be paid out of pocket, how the death benefit changes, and what happens if assumptions are lower than expected.

For clients attracted to personal banking concepts, this is where discipline matters. The strategy depends on design, funding, behavior, and review. It should be tested against less favorable conditions and compared with the client's need for liquidity outside the policy.

Surrender, Withdrawal, Loan: Not the Same Decision

Clients sometimes use the words access, borrow, cash out, and withdraw as if they mean the same thing. In a policy review, those words should be separated. Surrendering a policy usually means giving up the coverage in exchange for available surrender value, subject to contract terms. A withdrawal may remove value and reduce the death benefit. A policy loan may allow access while the policy remains in force, but interest accrues and the loan can affect future values.

Each option has a different consequence. The best choice depends on why money is needed, whether protection is still important, whether there are tax concerns, and whether the policy can support the transaction. A client using cash value for a small temporary need may need a different approach than a client considering repeated retirement income withdrawals.

Kayla's review can help slow this decision down so the client understands the tradeoffs before acting.

Reflection for Your Notes

As you think about cash value, policy loans, and important tradeoffs, write down what feels settled and what still feels unclear. A protection review is not about proving that you already know the answer. It is about bringing the right questions into the room so the next step is based on your life, your people, your budget, and your priorities.

Chapter 11: Life Insurance for Retirement and Safe Money Conversations

Start With the Human Need

Retirement planning is not only about reaching a date on the calendar. It is about creating income, managing risk, protecting a spouse, preparing for care needs, and deciding what kind of legacy should remain. Life insurance may belong in that conversation, but only when the purpose is clear.

In a healthy planning conversation, where protection meets income planning is the starting point. The goal is not to make anyone anxious or to make a product sound perfect. The goal is to understand what the coverage is supposed to protect, how long that need may last, and what tradeoffs are reasonable for the household.

Protection planning is not about fear. It is about giving the people you love more room to breathe if income, health, debt, business responsibilities, or family needs change unexpectedly.

A policy may be part of the answer, but the policy should follow the purpose. Clear goals make the product conversation calmer, more useful, and easier to review over time.

How the Concept Works

At its simplest, life insurance for retirement and safe money conversations is about connecting protection with retirement conversations without confusing the purpose. That does not mean every solution is simple. It means the purpose can be stated in ordinary language before the details begin.

Life insurance products are contracts, so premiums, underwriting, riders, exclusions, limitations, state availability, and policy terms all matter. The details should support the family goal instead of overwhelming it.

Some coverage is designed to last for a specific period. Some coverage is designed to last longer if premiums are paid and the policy stays in force. Some policies may build cash value. Some may include riders that can help during qualifying illness events. Some products are built for protection only, while others may cross into retirement income, safe money, or legacy conversations.

Nearing retirement, Sheila wants less market volatility and more predictable income options, while still keeping family protection in mind.

Important Nuance

Retirement income planning may involve Social Security timing, pensions, savings, annuities, life insurance, investments, taxes, inflation, health care costs, and legacy goals. Life insurance can be part of that conversation, but it should not be forced into a role it cannot responsibly fill.

Safe money strategies often focus on protecting principal, creating predictable income, reducing market exposure, or coordinating guarantees. Insurance and annuity guarantees depend on the financial strength and claims-paying ability of the issuing carrier.

The retirement conversation should compare liquidity, access, surrender periods, tax treatment, income needs, beneficiary goals, and what happens under less favorable assumptions.

A Familiar Situation

In an early conversation, it is normal not to know which type of coverage belongs in the discussion. The review should begin with the need, then narrow the options from there.

The better question is not simply what can be purchased today. The better question is what problem the coverage is supposed to solve and how the family would actually use it later.

One common misunderstanding is that life insurance is a retirement plan by itself. This belief can cause people to either delay planning or overcorrect with a decision that does not fit.

Where Confusion Begins

Another misunderstanding is that life insurance for retirement and safe money conversations can be judged by one feature alone. People may focus only on premium, only on cash value, only on the death benefit, only on a rider, or only on a story they heard from someone else. Those details matter, but they need context.

Another common mistake is assuming the planning is finished once a policy is placed. Life changes, employer benefits change, beneficiaries become outdated, and some policies need attention to stay aligned with the original goal.

What people often overlook with life insurance for retirement and safe money conversations is the family conversation around it. Someone may need to know where documents are kept, who to call, what the intended purpose is, and whether there are special family dynamics to consider.

The Overlooked Pieces

Ownership and beneficiary choices deserve careful attention. The policy owner controls the contract, the insured is the person covered, and the beneficiary receives the death benefit if the policy pays.

Timing also matters. Waiting can affect insurability, premium, and available options, while moving too quickly can create regret if the policy does not match the goal.

A protection review usually looks at income needs, risk tolerance, liquidity, guarantees, taxes, health, beneficiaries, and whether insurance products are suitable. It may also compare existing coverage with current goals and identify gaps that are not obvious from policy pages alone.

Review Questions to Bring Forward

A review may include income replacement, final expenses, mortgage protection, children, aging parents, business obligations, retirement timing, health considerations, and beneficiary updates.

The review should also ask what you do not want. Some people want temporary low-cost coverage, some want lifelong protection, some want to explore cash value carefully, and some want to avoid complexity.

If this sounds like your situation, mark the section and bring your questions to a protection review.

The Main Point

The main lesson of this chapter is that life insurance for retirement and safe money conversations should be discussed with patience and context. A policy is only useful when it supports the real-life purpose behind it.

There is no single answer that fits every family. The right conversation considers need, time horizon, budget, health, product design, and future review.

As you continue, keep asking one simple question: what would this coverage help my family preserve, avoid, or complete?

Looking Ahead

The next chapter turns to long-term care, chronic illness, and protection gaps, continuing the same theme: protection planning works best when the product discussion follows the human need.

Keeping the Retirement Purpose Clear

Life insurance sometimes appears in retirement conversations because protection, income, taxes, legacy, and care needs overlap. A person approaching retirement may want to protect a spouse, leave a legacy, create supplemental flexibility, or reduce exposure to market volatility. Those are legitimate topics, but the product discussion should remain grounded in suitability.

Annuities and certain insurance strategies may be used in safe money conversations because they can offer guarantees, income features, or protection from direct market loss, depending on the product. Those guarantees depend on the financial strength and claims-paying ability of the issuing carrier. Surrender charges, liquidity limits, rider costs, tax treatment, and income rules must be reviewed before a decision is made.

Life insurance is not automatically a retirement plan. It may support a retirement plan when the client needs death benefit protection, legacy planning, cash value features, or a strategy that has been stress-tested carefully. It should be compared with other available tools, not presented as the only answer.

A Review Conversation Near Retirement

A review may ask whether a surviving spouse would have enough income, whether debts will be paid off, whether long-term care costs could disrupt the plan, whether existing policies still make sense, and whether beneficiaries are current. It may also look at how much liquidity should remain outside insurance products. The goal is not to chase a clever strategy. The goal is to protect retirement dignity and family choices.

Spouse Protection in Retirement

A retirement plan can look solid while both spouses are living and still become fragile after the first death. Pension choices, Social Security income, annuity income, required expenses, debts, and taxes may change. Life insurance may be reviewed as one possible way to provide liquidity or survivor support, depending on health, budget, and existing resources.

Safe money conversations may also include annuities or other insurance-based tools. The goal may be predictable income, principal protection from direct market loss, or a way to reduce pressure on other assets. These conversations require care because guarantees, liquidity limits, surrender charges, rider fees, and tax treatment vary.

A review with Kayla can help organize these questions without turning life insurance into a cure-all. The first issue is the client's retirement concern. Is it income, legacy, spouse protection, market risk, care costs, taxes, or something else? Once the concern is named, the tools can be compared more responsibly.

Legacy Versus Income

Retirement conversations often blend two desires: having enough income while living and leaving something meaningful behind. Those goals can support each other, but they can also compete. Money used to create income may not be available for legacy. Money preserved for heirs may not be available for care, emergencies, or a surviving spouse's comfort.

Life insurance may be reviewed when a client wants a defined legacy, spouse protection, or tax-sensitive transfer planning, but it should be coordinated with income needs. Annuities or other safe money tools may be reviewed when predictable income is the concern. The review should name the priority before comparing products.

A client who says, "I do not want to run out of money," may need a different conversation than a client who says, "I want my children to receive something." Many people want both. The planning work is deciding what balance is realistic.

Reflection for Your Notes

As you think about life insurance for retirement and safe money conversations, write down what feels settled and what still feels unclear. A protection review is not about proving that you already know the answer. It is about bringing the right questions into the room so the next step is based on your life, your people, your budget, and your priorities.

Chapter 12: Long-Term Care, Chronic Illness, and Protection Gaps

Why Families Pause Here

Care needs can change a family rhythm overnight. A spouse may become a caregiver. An adult child may reduce work hours. Savings may be redirected toward home help, transportation, or facility care. That is why chronic illness and long-term care conversations belong beside life insurance reviews.

In a healthy planning conversation, planning for care before the crisis is the starting point. The goal is not to make anyone anxious or to make a product sound perfect. The goal is to understand what the coverage is supposed to protect, how long that need may last, and what tradeoffs are reasonable for the household.

Protection planning is not about fear. It is about giving the people you love more room to breathe if income, health, debt, business responsibilities, or family needs change unexpectedly.

A policy may be part of the answer, but the policy should follow the purpose. Clear goals make the product conversation calmer, more useful, and easier to review over time.

What It Means

At its simplest, long-term care, chronic illness, and protection gaps is about seeing how care needs can affect income, savings, and family time. That does not mean every solution is simple. It means the purpose can be stated in ordinary language before the details begin.

Life insurance products are contracts, so premiums, underwriting, riders, exclusions, limitations, state availability, and policy terms all matter. The details should support the family goal instead of overwhelming it.

Some coverage is designed to last for a specific period. Some coverage is designed to last longer if premiums are paid and the

policy stays in force. Some policies may build cash value. Some may include riders that can help during qualifying illness events. Some products are built for protection only, while others may cross into retirement income, safe money, or legacy conversations.

When Mr. Lee needs help at home, his daughter discovers how quickly caregiving affects work schedules and household cash flow.

A Simple Example

In an early conversation, it is normal not to know which type of coverage belongs in the discussion. The review should begin with the need, then narrow the options from there.

The better question is not simply what can be purchased today. The better question is what problem the coverage is supposed to solve and how the family would actually use it later.

One common misunderstanding is that Medicare will handle every long-term care need. This belief can cause people to either delay planning or overcorrect with a decision that does not fit.

Common Assumptions

Another misunderstanding is that long-term care, chronic illness, and protection gaps can be judged by one feature alone. People may focus only on premium, only on cash value, only on the death benefit, only on a rider, or only on a story they heard from someone else. Those details matter, but they need context.

Another common mistake is assuming the planning is finished once a policy is placed. Life changes, employer benefits change, beneficiaries become outdated, and some policies need attention to stay aligned with the original goal.

What people often overlook with long-term care, chronic illness, and protection gaps is the family conversation around it. Someone may need to know where documents are kept, who to call, what the intended purpose is, and whether there are special family dynamics to consider.

What People Forget to Ask

Ownership and beneficiary choices deserve careful attention. The policy owner controls the contract, the insured is the person covered, and the beneficiary receives the death benefit if the policy pays.

Timing also matters. Waiting can affect insurability, premium, and available options, while moving too quickly can create regret if the policy does not match the goal.

A protection review usually looks at family caregiver capacity, income, assets, health history, available riders, dedicated coverage, and professional guidance. It may also compare existing coverage with current goals and identify gaps that are not obvious from policy pages alone.

What the Review May Explore

A review may include income replacement, final expenses, mortgage protection, children, aging parents, business obligations, retirement timing, health considerations, and beneficiary updates.

The review should also ask what you do not want. Some people want temporary low-cost coverage, some want lifelong protection, some want to explore cash value carefully, and some want to avoid complexity.

If this sounds like your situation, mark the section and bring your questions to a protection review.

A Practical Summary

The main lesson of this chapter is that long-term care, chronic illness, and protection gaps should be discussed with patience and context. A policy is only useful when it supports the real-life purpose behind it.

There is no single answer that fits every family. The right conversation considers need, time horizon, budget, health, product design, and future review.

As you continue, keep asking one simple question: what would this coverage help my family preserve, avoid, or complete?

Continue With This in Mind

The next chapter turns to beneficiaries, legacy, and family conversations, continuing the same theme: protection planning works best when the product discussion follows the human need.

The Cost of Care Is Also a Family Issue

Long-term care planning is not just a spreadsheet topic. Care can affect who drives to appointments, who manages medication, who misses work, and who pays for help. Some life insurance riders may help in qualifying circumstances, while dedicated long-term care planning may be needed in other situations.

A review can help families discuss what resources exist, what assumptions may be unrealistic, and how care needs could affect retirement income and legacy goals.

The Caregiver Conversation

Many families assume care will somehow be handled by love alone. Love matters, but care also requires time, money, coordination, and stamina. An adult child may live far away. A spouse may have health limitations. A family member may want to help but be unable to leave work. These realities should be discussed before care is needed.

A protection review can ask where care would ideally happen, who could realistically provide help, what income would be affected, and what resources could pay for assistance. It can also explore whether existing policies include chronic illness or long-term care riders and whether dedicated long-term care planning should be considered.

This is not about predicting every future medical need. It is about not pretending the risk belongs to someone else. When care needs arrive, families often wish they had talked sooner.

Reflection for Your Notes

As you think about long-term care, chronic illness, and protection gaps, write down what feels settled and what still feels unclear. A protection review is not about proving that you already know the answer. It is about bringing the right questions into the room so the next step is based on your life, your people, your budget, and your priorities.

Chapter 13: Beneficiaries, Legacy, and Family Conversations

Why This Matters Now

Beneficiary planning looks simple until real life gets involved. Marriage, divorce, remarriage, minor children, blended families, estrangement, death, business ownership, and old paperwork can all turn a simple form into an important planning issue.

In a healthy planning conversation, making intentions easier to follow is the starting point. The goal is not to make anyone anxious or to make a product sound perfect. The goal is to understand what the coverage is supposed to protect, how long that need may last, and what tradeoffs are reasonable for the household.

Protection planning is not about fear. It is about giving the people you love more room to breathe if income, health, debt, business responsibilities, or family needs change unexpectedly.

A policy may be part of the answer, but the policy should follow the purpose. Clear goals make the product conversation calmer, more useful, and easier to review over time.

The Simple Explanation

At its simplest, beneficiaries, legacy, and family conversations is about helping the right people receive resources with less confusion. That does not mean every solution is simple. It means the purpose can be stated in ordinary language before the details begin.

Life insurance products are contracts, so premiums, underwriting, riders, exclusions, limitations, state availability, and policy terms all matter. The details should support the family goal instead of overwhelming it.

Some coverage is designed to last for a specific period. Some coverage is designed to last longer if premiums are paid and the policy stays in force. Some policies may build cash value. Some

may include riders that can help during qualifying illness events. Some products are built for protection only, while others may cross into retirement income, safe money, or legacy conversations.

A policy still names an ex-spouse because nobody reviewed the beneficiary form after a divorce and remarriage.

Important Nuance

Beneficiary designations deserve attention because they can direct where policy proceeds go. This book does not provide legal advice, and complex beneficiary decisions should be reviewed with qualified counsel, especially when minor children, blended families, special needs planning, trusts, estates, divorce, or creditor concerns are involved.

A beneficiary review should include primary and contingent beneficiaries. It should also ask whether the named people are still living, whether names are spelled correctly, whether percentages add up properly, and whether the designation still reflects current wishes.

Family conversations can be simple. They do not have to reveal every dollar amount. Sometimes the most helpful message is, "I have coverage, I have named beneficiaries, and these are the people to contact if something happens."

A Client-Style Scenario

In an early conversation, it is normal not to know which type of coverage belongs in the discussion. The review should begin with the need, then narrow the options from there.

The better question is not simply what can be purchased today. The better question is what problem the coverage is supposed to solve and how the family would actually use it later.

One common misunderstanding is that a will automatically controls every life insurance beneficiary. This belief can cause people to either delay planning or overcorrect with a decision that does not fit.

What Gets Misunderstood

Another misunderstanding is that beneficiaries, legacy, and family conversations can be judged by one feature alone. People may focus only on premium, only on cash value, only on the death benefit, only on a rider, or only on a story they heard from someone else. Those details matter, but they need context.

Another common mistake is assuming the planning is finished once a policy is placed. Life changes, employer benefits change, beneficiaries become outdated, and some policies need attention to stay aligned with the original goal.

What people often overlook with beneficiaries, legacy, and family conversations is the family conversation around it. Someone may need to know where documents are kept, who to call, what the intended purpose is, and whether there are special family dynamics to consider.

What Often Gets Missed

Ownership and beneficiary choices deserve careful attention. The policy owner controls the contract, the insured is the person covered, and the beneficiary receives the death benefit if the policy pays.

Timing also matters. Waiting can affect insurability, premium, and available options, while moving too quickly can create regret if the policy does not match the goal.

A protection review usually looks at primary and contingent beneficiaries, minor children, trusts or estate questions for counsel, updates after life events, and family communication. It may also compare existing coverage with current goals and identify gaps that are not obvious from policy pages alone.

Inside a Thoughtful Review

A review may include income replacement, final expenses, mortgage protection, children, aging parents, business obligations, retirement timing, health considerations, and beneficiary updates.

The review should also ask what you do not want. Some people want temporary low-cost coverage, some want lifelong protection, some want to explore cash value carefully, and some want to avoid complexity.

If this sounds like your situation, mark the section and bring your questions to a protection review.

Chapter Summary

The main lesson of this chapter is that beneficiaries, legacy, and family conversations should be discussed with patience and context. A policy is only useful when it supports the real-life purpose behind it.

There is no single answer that fits every family. The right conversation considers need, time horizon, budget, health, product design, and future review.

As you continue, keep asking one simple question: what would this coverage help my family preserve, avoid, or complete?

Next Conversation

The next chapter turns to business owner and key person protection basics, continuing the same theme: protection planning works best when the product discussion follows the human need.

When a Form Carries a Family Story

Beneficiary forms can look administrative, but they often carry the weight of family relationships. A divorced parent may forget to update an old policy. A remarried spouse may assume everything is handled. A grandparent may name a minor child without understanding how proceeds may need to be managed. A business owner may name a person when an agreement points somewhere else.

This book cannot provide legal advice, and complex beneficiary planning should involve qualified legal counsel. Still, every client can understand the importance of reviewing names, percentages, contingent beneficiaries, and the practical effect of the current designation. A beneficiary form should be consistent with the client's current intentions and coordinated with broader planning where appropriate.

Legacy conversations do not have to be dramatic. Sometimes they begin with simple clarity: who should be contacted, where policies are kept, which professional relationships matter, and what the coverage is intended to accomplish. Families often feel calmer when they know there is a plan, even if every detail remains private.

Review Questions for Beneficiary Planning

Ask whether your beneficiary choices still match your life today. Have you married, divorced, remarried, had a child, lost a loved one, started a business, created a trust, or taken on caregiving responsibilities? Are contingent beneficiaries named? Are minor children involved? Do you need legal guidance before naming a trust or estate? These are review questions, not legal conclusions.

Blended Families and Minor Children

Blended families and minor children deserve special attention. A client may love everyone involved and still need precise planning. Naming a minor child directly may create complications because a child generally cannot manage proceeds. Naming a new spouse may be appropriate in one family and create conflict in another. Naming an estate may have consequences that should be reviewed with legal counsel.

The insurance review should not replace legal advice, but it can identify when legal advice is needed. If a client mentions a trust, special needs beneficiary, estranged family member, divorce decree, business partner, or desire to control how money is used, the conversation should slow down.

Legacy planning is not only about leaving money. It is about leaving less confusion. Updated beneficiaries, clear records, and professional coordination can spare loved ones from uncertainty at the worst possible time.

The Conversation Without the Dollar Amounts

Some clients avoid family conversations because they do not want to disclose private financial details. That is understandable. Legacy communication does not always require sharing dollar amounts. A client can tell a trusted person where documents are stored, which advisor to contact, whether policies exist, and whether beneficiary forms have been reviewed.

This simple communication can prevent confusion. Loved ones may not know which company holds a policy, whether coverage is individual or through work, or whether a policy has lapsed. They may not know if there are business policies, child policies, or old policies from decades ago.

A review can help create a short information list without turning the client's private finances into a family meeting. The goal is not oversharing. The goal is making sure important protection is findable when it matters.

Reviewing After Life Changes

Beneficiary reviews are especially important after marriage, divorce, birth, adoption, death, remarriage, estrangement, business changes, and major financial changes. These events can change who should receive funds, who should manage funds, and whether professional legal guidance is needed. The policy may still be good while the beneficiary form is outdated.

A review does not have to solve every legal question. It can identify the questions that should be taken to an attorney or tax professional. It can also confirm simple details such as spelling, contact information, contingent beneficiaries, and whether percentages add up properly. Small corrections can prevent large confusion later.

Reflection for Your Notes

As you think about beneficiaries, legacy, and family conversations, write down what feels settled and what still feels unclear. A protection review is not about proving that you already know the answer. It is about bringing the right questions into the room so the next step is based on your life, your people, your budget, and your priorities.

Chapter 14: Business Owner and Key Person Protection Basics

The Real-Life Reason

A small business often depends on a few people more than anyone realizes. The owner may be the rainmaker, signer, guarantor, technician, relationship holder, or payroll problem-solver. If that person is gone or seriously ill, the business may need cash and a plan very quickly.

In a healthy planning conversation, protecting the people behind the business is the starting point. The goal is not to make anyone anxious or to make a product sound perfect. The goal is to understand what the coverage is supposed to protect, how long that need may last, and what tradeoffs are reasonable for the household.

Protection planning is not about fear. It is about giving the people you love more room to breathe if income, health, debt, business responsibilities, or family needs change unexpectedly.

A policy may be part of the answer, but the policy should follow the purpose. Clear goals make the product conversation calmer, more useful, and easier to review over time.

Plain English First

At its simplest, business owner and key person protection basics is about keeping a business, family, partner, or employee group from being blindsided. That does not mean every solution is simple. It means the purpose can be stated in ordinary language before the details begin.

Life insurance products are contracts, so premiums, underwriting, riders, exclusions, limitations, state availability, and policy terms all matter. The details should support the family goal instead of overwhelming it.

Some coverage is designed to last for a specific period. Some coverage is designed to last longer if premiums are paid and the policy stays in force. Some policies may build cash value. Some may include riders that can help during qualifying illness events. Some products are built for protection only, while others may cross into retirement income, safe money, or legacy conversations.

A small contractor depends on one lead estimator and one owner relationship with the bank. A planning review reveals more than personal coverage needs.

How This Can Show Up

In an early conversation, it is normal not to know which type of coverage belongs in the discussion. The review should begin with the need, then narrow the options from there.

The better question is not simply what can be purchased today. The better question is what problem the coverage is supposed to solve and how the family would actually use it later.

One common misunderstanding is that business coverage is only for large companies. This belief can cause people to either delay planning or overcorrect with a decision that does not fit.

A Common Misread

Another misunderstanding is that business owner and key person protection basics can be judged by one feature alone. People may focus only on premium, only on cash value, only on the death benefit, only on a rider, or only on a story they heard from someone else. Those details matter, but they need context.

Another common mistake is assuming the planning is finished once a policy is placed. Life changes, employer benefits change, beneficiaries become outdated, and some policies need attention to stay aligned with the original goal.

What people often overlook with business owner and key person protection basics is the family conversation around it. Someone may need to know where documents are kept, who to call, what the intended purpose is, and whether there are special family dynamics to consider.

The Quiet Details

Ownership and beneficiary choices deserve careful attention. The policy owner controls the contract, the insured is the person covered, and the beneficiary receives the death benefit if the policy pays.

Timing also matters. Waiting can affect insurability, premium, and available options, while moving too quickly can create regret if the policy does not match the goal.

A protection review usually looks at key person risk, buy-sell funding, debt obligations, payroll continuity, ownership, beneficiary structure, and tax/legal coordination. It may also compare existing coverage with current goals and identify gaps that are not obvious from policy pages alone.

What an Advisor Looks For

A review may include income replacement, final expenses, mortgage protection, children, aging parents, business obligations, retirement timing, health considerations, and beneficiary updates.

The review should also ask what you do not want. Some people want temporary low-cost coverage, some want lifelong protection, some want to explore cash value carefully, and some want to avoid complexity.

If this sounds like your situation, mark the section and bring your questions to a protection review.

In Short

The main lesson of this chapter is that business owner and key person protection basics should be discussed with patience and context. A policy is only useful when it supports the real-life purpose behind it.

There is no single answer that fits every family. The right conversation considers need, time horizon, budget, health, product design, and future review.

As you continue, keep asking one simple question: what would this coverage help my family preserve, avoid, or complete?

A Soft Step Forward

The next chapter turns to common life insurance and legacy planning mistakes, continuing the same theme: protection planning works best when the product discussion follows the human need.

The Business Risk Behind the Family Risk

For business owners, personal and business protection often overlap. The same person may provide household income, sign business loans, manage client relationships, supervise employees, and keep operations moving. If that person dies or becomes seriously ill, the family may lose income while the business loses leadership and cash flow.

Key person insurance may help a business survive the loss of a critical employee or owner. Buy-sell funding may help partners transfer ownership according to an agreement. Coverage tied to business debt may help protect collateral, credit relationships, or family assets. None of these ideas should be implemented casually. Ownership, beneficiary structure, tax questions, legal agreements, and business valuation should be coordinated with qualified professionals.

Small businesses need this conversation just as much as large companies. A two-person firm can be deeply vulnerable. A solo owner may need a plan for outstanding invoices, payroll, client communication, equipment loans, and family income. The right review begins with how the business actually runs.

What Kayla May Want to Understand

A business protection review may ask who can sign checks, who can sell, who can estimate jobs, who holds licenses, who guarantees debt, and what would happen in the first thirty to ninety days after a death or serious illness. It may also ask whether there is a written buy-sell agreement, whether the funding matches the agreement, and whether personal coverage is separate from business coverage.

Personal Coverage Is Not Always Enough

A business owner may have personal life insurance and still have business exposure. Personal coverage may be intended for the spouse and children, while the business needs cash for payroll, debt, recruiting, training, or buying out an ownership interest. Mixing those purposes without a plan can create conflict.

For example, if a family receives personal death benefit proceeds but the business loan is also pressing, should the family use personal money to protect the company? If a partner needs to buy out the deceased owner's share, is there a funded agreement? If a key employee dies, does the business have enough cash to survive the transition?

These questions often require coordination with an attorney, tax professional, and business advisor. Kayla's role can include helping identify the insurance questions and making sure the coverage discussion lines up with the business reality.

The First Ninety Days

A useful business protection exercise is to imagine the first ninety days after the owner or key person is gone. Who notifies clients? Who talks to the bank? Who signs payroll? Who has passwords? Who can finish open jobs, collect receivables, and manage vendor relationships? Who explains the situation to employees?

Insurance cannot answer every operational question, but it may provide cash while those questions are being handled. That cash may help hire temporary help, recruit a replacement, pay debt, fund a buyout, or give the family time to decide whether to continue or sell.

This is why business owner coverage should be reviewed alongside business documents. A policy without an agreement may create confusion. An agreement without funding may be difficult to carry out. A review can identify the gap and point the client toward the right professional coordination.

Reflection for Your Notes

As you think about business owner and key person protection basics, write down what feels settled and what still feels unclear. A protection review is not about proving that you already know the answer. It is about bringing the right questions into the room so the next step is based on your life, your people, your budget, and your priorities.

Chapter 15: Common Life Insurance and Legacy Planning Mistakes

Start With the Human Need

Most protection mistakes are quiet. They do not happen because someone is careless. They happen because life changes and the old plan does not keep up.

In a healthy planning conversation, avoiding quiet gaps is the starting point. The goal is not to make anyone anxious or to make a product sound perfect. The goal is to understand what the coverage is supposed to protect, how long that need may last, and what tradeoffs are reasonable for the household.

Protection planning is not about fear. It is about giving the people you love more room to breathe if income, health, debt, business responsibilities, or family needs change unexpectedly.

A policy may be part of the answer, but the policy should follow the purpose. Clear goals make the product conversation calmer, more useful, and easier to review over time.

How the Concept Works

At its simplest, common life insurance and legacy planning mistakes is about spotting old assumptions before they become family problems. That does not mean every solution is simple. It means the purpose can be stated in ordinary language before the details begin.

Life insurance products are contracts, so premiums, underwriting, riders, exclusions, limitations, state availability, and policy terms all matter. The details should support the family goal instead of overwhelming it.

Some coverage is designed to last for a specific period. Some coverage is designed to last longer if premiums are paid and the policy stays in force. Some policies may build cash value. Some may include riders that can help during qualifying illness events.

Some products are built for protection only, while others may cross into retirement income, safe money, or legacy conversations.

Nina has three policies, but one is near lapse, one has an outdated beneficiary, and one no longer matches her income needs.

A Familiar Situation

In an early conversation, it is normal not to know which type of coverage belongs in the discussion. The review should begin with the need, then narrow the options from there.

The better question is not simply what can be purchased today. The better question is what problem the coverage is supposed to solve and how the family would actually use it later.

One common misunderstanding is that having something means having enough. This belief can cause people to either delay planning or overcorrect with a decision that does not fit.

Where Confusion Begins

Another misunderstanding is that common life insurance and legacy planning mistakes can be judged by one feature alone. People may focus only on premium, only on cash value, only on the death benefit, only on a rider, or only on a story they heard from someone else. Those details matter, but they need context.

Another common mistake is assuming the planning is finished once a policy is placed. Life changes, employer benefits change, beneficiaries become outdated, and some policies need attention to stay aligned with the original goal.

What people often overlook with common life insurance and legacy planning mistakes is the family conversation around it. Someone may need to know where documents are kept, who to call, what the intended purpose is, and whether there are special family dynamics to consider.

The Overlooked Pieces

Ownership and beneficiary choices deserve careful attention. The policy owner controls the contract, the insured is the person covered, and the beneficiary receives the death benefit if the policy pays.

Timing also matters. Waiting can affect insurability, premium, and available options, while moving too quickly can create regret if the policy does not match the goal.

A protection review usually looks at coverage amounts, policy health, beneficiaries, ownership, affordability, and new risks since the last review. It may also compare existing coverage with current goals and identify gaps that are not obvious from policy pages alone.

Review Questions to Bring Forward

A review may include income replacement, final expenses, mortgage protection, children, aging parents, business obligations, retirement timing, health considerations, and beneficiary updates.

The review should also ask what you do not want. Some people want temporary low-cost coverage, some want lifelong protection, some want to explore cash value carefully, and some want to avoid complexity.

If this sounds like your situation, mark the section and bring your questions to a protection review.

The Main Point

The main lesson of this chapter is that common life insurance and legacy planning mistakes should be discussed with patience and context. A policy is only useful when it supports the real-life purpose behind it.

There is no single answer that fits every family. The right conversation considers need, time horizon, budget, health, product design, and future review.

As you continue, keep asking one simple question: what would this coverage help my family preserve, avoid, or complete?

Looking Ahead

The next chapter turns to what to gather before a protection review, continuing the same theme: protection planning works best when the product discussion follows the human need.

Small Oversights, Big Consequences

Common mistakes include relying only on workplace coverage, forgetting to update beneficiaries, assuming old policies still perform as expected, buying coverage without naming the purpose, or letting affordability problems grow quietly. None of these mistakes mean a person failed. They mean the plan needs attention.

A review after marriage, divorce, birth, death, home purchase, business change, retirement, or major financial change can catch issues before the family has to discover them during a crisis.

Why Reviews Catch What Memory Misses

People often remember buying a policy but forget the details. They may not remember the term length, conversion deadline, beneficiary, loan balance, premium schedule, or whether living benefits were included. A review brings those details back into view.

Another common mistake is assuming health will always allow new coverage later. Underwriting can change the options available. Waiting may still be reasonable in some situations, but it should be an informed choice rather than a default caused by avoidance.

The most repairable mistake is silence. Families do not need every detail, but someone should know that coverage exists and where to find information. Silence can turn a good policy into a harder claim experience.

Reflection for Your Notes

As you think about common life insurance and legacy planning mistakes, write down what feels settled and what still feels unclear. A protection review is not about proving that you already know the answer. It is about bringing the right questions into the room so the next step is based on your life, your people, your budget, and your priorities.

Chapter 16: What to Gather Before a Protection Review

Why Families Pause Here

A protection review feels easier when the conversation starts with real information instead of guesses. You do not need a perfect file folder, but a few documents can help Kayla see what is already in place and what may need attention.

In a healthy planning conversation, making the conversation easier is the starting point. The goal is not to make anyone anxious or to make a product sound perfect. The goal is to understand what the coverage is supposed to protect, how long that need may last, and what tradeoffs are reasonable for the household.

Protection planning is not about fear. It is about giving the people you love more room to breathe if income, health, debt, business responsibilities, or family needs change unexpectedly.

A policy may be part of the answer, but the policy should follow the purpose. Clear goals make the product conversation calmer, more useful, and easier to review over time.

What It Means

At its simplest, what to gather before a protection review is about bringing enough information to make the review practical. That does not mean every solution is simple. It means the purpose can be stated in ordinary language before the details begin.

Life insurance products are contracts, so premiums, underwriting, riders, exclusions, limitations, state availability, and policy terms all matter. The details should support the family goal instead of overwhelming it.

Some coverage is designed to last for a specific period. Some coverage is designed to last longer if premiums are paid and the policy stays in force. Some policies may build cash value. Some may include riders that can help during qualifying illness events.

Some products are built for protection only, while others may cross into retirement income, safe money, or legacy conversations.

Before meeting with Kayla, a family gathers policies, a mortgage statement, an employer benefit summary, and a list of questions.

Important Nuance

Protection review checklist: current life insurance policies; workplace benefit summaries; mortgage or debt information; income estimates; household budget comfort range; beneficiary forms; retirement account beneficiary information; business agreements if applicable; and questions you want answered.

It is also helpful to list major life changes: marriage, divorce, birth or adoption, death in the family, home purchase, job change, business launch, business sale, retirement, health diagnosis, caregiving responsibility, or major financial change.

You do not need perfection before scheduling a review. Bring what you have. A good review can identify what is missing and help you request documents from carriers, employers, or other professionals.

A Simple Example

In an early conversation, it is normal not to know which type of coverage belongs in the discussion. The review should begin with the need, then narrow the options from there.

The better question is not simply what can be purchased today. The better question is what problem the coverage is supposed to solve and how the family would actually use it later.

One common misunderstanding is that a review requires every document before the first conversation. This belief can cause people to either delay planning or overcorrect with a decision that does not fit.

Common Assumptions

Another misunderstanding is that what to gather before a protection review can be judged by one feature alone. People may focus only on premium, only on cash value, only on the death benefit, only on a rider, or only on a story they heard from someone else. Those details matter, but they need context.

Another common mistake is assuming the planning is finished once a policy is placed. Life changes, employer benefits change, beneficiaries become outdated, and some policies need attention to stay aligned with the original goal.

What people often overlook with what to gather before a protection review is the family conversation around it. Someone may need to know where documents are kept, who to call, what the intended purpose is, and whether there are special family dynamics to consider.

What People Forget to Ask

Ownership and beneficiary choices deserve careful attention. The policy owner controls the contract, the insured is the person covered, and the beneficiary receives the death benefit if the policy pays.

Timing also matters. Waiting can affect insurability, premium, and available options, while moving too quickly can create regret if the policy does not match the goal.

A protection review usually looks at current policies, workplace benefits, debts, income, dependents, goals, health considerations, and questions. It may also compare existing coverage with current goals and identify gaps that are not obvious from policy pages alone.

What the Review May Explore

A review may include income replacement, final expenses, mortgage protection, children, aging parents, business obligations, retirement timing, health considerations, and beneficiary updates.

The review should also ask what you do not want. Some people want temporary low-cost coverage, some want lifelong protection, some want to explore cash value carefully, and some want to avoid complexity.

If this sounds like your situation, mark the section and bring your questions to a protection review.

A Practical Summary

The main lesson of this chapter is that what to gather before a protection review should be discussed with patience and context. A policy is only useful when it supports the real-life purpose behind it.

There is no single answer that fits every family. The right conversation considers need, time horizon, budget, health, product design, and future review.

As you continue, keep asking one simple question: what would this coverage help my family preserve, avoid, or complete?

Continue With This in Mind

The next chapter turns to how price services group can help, continuing the same theme: protection planning works best when the product discussion follows the human need.

The Practical Checklist

☐ Bring what you have, even if it is incomplete. Useful documents may include current life insurance statements, employer benefit summaries, mortgage statements, business loan information, retirement account beneficiary confirmations, annuity statements, long-term care or disability coverage information, and any recent letters from insurance carriers.

☐ It also helps to bring your questions. You might ask whether your coverage is enough, whether workplace insurance is portable, whether an old policy is still healthy, whether a child policy makes sense, whether living benefits are included, whether your beneficiaries are current, or whether retirement income planning should be reviewed alongside life insurance.

☐ A review also benefits from context. Share major life events such as marriage, divorce, birth, adoption, death in the family, home purchase, job change, retirement, business growth, sale of a business, new caregiving responsibilities, or a health diagnosis. These events do not automatically mean you need a new policy, but they often mean the old plan deserves a fresh look.

If You Cannot Find Everything

☐ Do not cancel a review because one document is missing. Start with what you know. Kayla can help identify what to request from an employer, carrier, or other professional. The purpose of the first conversation is not to grade your paperwork. It is to understand your life well enough to make the next step clearer.

Organizing Without Overwhelming Yourself

☐ If gathering documents feels like too much, start with four categories: what you own, what you owe, who depends on you, and what has changed. What you own includes policies, workplace benefits, retirement accounts, annuities, and savings. What you owe includes mortgage, business debt, personal loans, and obligations you would not want to leave unmanaged. Who depends on you includes spouse, children, parents, business partners, employees, or anyone else affected by your income or care.

☐ What has changed may be the most important category. A marriage, divorce, birth, death, home purchase, retirement, health change, new business, or caregiving role can make an old plan outdated. Bring those updates even if you cannot find every document.

☐ A good review turns incomplete information into a next-step list. It should make the client feel more organized, not embarrassed.

A Simple One-Page Snapshot

☐ Before the review, it can help to make a one-page snapshot. Write down household members, approximate income, major debts, employer benefits, existing policies, business interests, caregiving responsibilities, and recent life changes. Do not worry about making it perfect. The snapshot gives the conversation a map.

☐ Next, write three questions you want answered. They might be: Is my work coverage enough? Should I keep this old policy? Do my beneficiaries still make sense? Would living benefits help my family? How does life insurance connect to retirement income? Should my business have key person coverage?

☐ This preparation keeps the meeting practical. It also helps Kayla focus on what matters most to you instead of guessing from documents alone.

Reflection for Your Notes

☐ As you think about what to gather before a protection review, write down what feels settled and what still feels unclear. A protection review is not about proving that you already know the answer. It is about bringing the right questions into the room so the next step is based on your life, your people, your budget, and your priorities.

Chapter 17: How Price Services Group Can Help

Why This Matters Now

Price Services Group helps clients turn scattered questions into a clearer protection conversation. The process is not designed to pressure people into a product. It is designed to help them understand what they have, what they may be missing, and what options may fit the next step.

In a healthy planning conversation, guidance with room to breathe is the starting point. The goal is not to make anyone anxious or to make a product sound perfect. The goal is to understand what the coverage is supposed to protect, how long that need may last, and what tradeoffs are reasonable for the household.

Protection planning is not about fear. It is about giving the people you love more room to breathe if income, health, debt, business responsibilities, or family needs change unexpectedly.

A policy may be part of the answer, but the policy should follow the purpose. Clear goals make the product conversation calmer, more useful, and easier to review over time.

The Simple Explanation

At its simplest, how price services group can help is about organizing questions and comparing options without rushing the decision. That does not mean every solution is simple. It means the purpose can be stated in ordinary language before the details begin.

Life insurance products are contracts, so premiums, underwriting, riders, exclusions, limitations, state availability, and policy terms all matter. The details should support the family goal instead of overwhelming it.

Some coverage is designed to last for a specific period. Some coverage is designed to last longer if premiums are paid and the policy stays in force. Some policies may build cash value. Some

may include riders that can help during qualifying illness events. Some products are built for protection only, while others may cross into retirement income, safe money, or legacy conversations.

A client arrives unsure whether to keep an old policy, add term coverage, or consider permanent insurance. The conversation starts with goals, not products.

Important Nuance

Price Services Group, L.L.C. can help clients review existing coverage, identify possible protection gaps, compare educational options, and discuss whether term life, whole life, universal life, indexed universal life, final expense, mortgage protection, children's coverage, living benefits, long-term care planning, retirement income planning, safe money strategies, business owner protection, or beneficiary planning should be part of the conversation.

The role of the guide is to ask better questions, explain options clearly, and help you move at a pace that respects your family. The phrase Where You Matter is not just a tagline; it is a reminder that the client is not a transaction.

If you would like help reviewing your current coverage, retirement income plan, life insurance, or protection gaps, you can schedule a personalized conversation: https://host.safemsngr.com/widget/bookings/psglifeandretirementplan

A Client-Style Scenario

In an early conversation, it is normal not to know which type of coverage belongs in the discussion. The review should begin with the need, then narrow the options from there.

The better question is not simply what can be purchased today. The better question is what problem the coverage is supposed to solve and how the family would actually use it later.

One common misunderstanding is that an advisor's job is to push one product. This belief can cause people to either delay planning or overcorrect with a decision that does not fit.

What Gets Misunderstood

Another misunderstanding is that how price services group can help can be judged by one feature alone. People may focus only on premium, only on cash value, only on the death benefit, only on a rider, or only on a story they heard from someone else. Those details matter, but they need context.

Another common mistake is assuming the planning is finished once a policy is placed. Life changes, employer benefits change, beneficiaries become outdated, and some policies need attention to stay aligned with the original goal.

What people often overlook with how price services group can help is the family conversation around it. Someone may need to know where documents are kept, who to call, what the intended purpose is, and whether there are special family dynamics to consider.

What Often Gets Missed

Ownership and beneficiary choices deserve careful attention. The policy owner controls the contract, the insured is the person covered, and the beneficiary receives the death benefit if the policy pays.

Timing also matters. Waiting can affect insurability, premium, and available options, while moving too quickly can create regret if the policy does not match the goal.

A protection review usually looks at needs, timing, budget, existing coverage, suitability, carrier options, and follow-up service. It may also compare existing coverage with current goals and identify gaps that are not obvious from policy pages alone.

Inside a Thoughtful Review

A review may include income replacement, final expenses, mortgage protection, children, aging parents, business obligations, retirement timing, health considerations, and beneficiary updates.

The review should also ask what you do not want. Some people want temporary low-cost coverage, some want lifelong protection, some want to explore cash value carefully, and some want to avoid complexity.

If this sounds like your situation, mark the section and bring your questions to a protection review.

Chapter Summary

The main lesson of this chapter is that how price services group can help should be discussed with patience and context. A policy is only useful when it supports the real-life purpose behind it.

There is no single answer that fits every family. The right conversation considers need, time horizon, budget, health, product design, and future review.

As you continue, keep asking one simple question: what would this coverage help my family preserve, avoid, or complete?

Next Conversation

The next chapter turns to about the author, continuing the same theme: protection planning works best when the product discussion follows the human need.

The Price Services Group Approach

Price Services Group begins with listening. Before talking about term life, whole life, universal life, indexed universal life, final expense, mortgage protection, children's whole life, living benefits, long-term care planning, retirement income planning, safe money strategies, beneficiary planning, legacy planning, business owner protection, or family protection, the conversation should identify what the client is trying to protect.

That may include reviewing current policies, explaining policy language, comparing educational options, helping clients understand gaps, and coordinating questions for legal, tax, estate planning, investment, insurance, or retirement professionals where appropriate. The firm does not need to make the conversation complicated to make it valuable.

The phrase Where You Matter is a service standard. It means the client is allowed to ask basic questions. It means pace matters. It means recommendations should be explained in ordinary language. It means the plan should respect budget, suitability, family priorities, and future review.

A Soft Invitation

If you would like help reviewing your current coverage, retirement income plan, life insurance, or protection gaps, you can schedule a personalized conversation: https://host.safemsngr.com/widget/bookings/psglifeandretirementplan

You do not need to know exactly what you need before scheduling. The conversation can begin with what you have, what has changed, and what you want your family to be able to count on.

What the First Conversation Can Cover

A first conversation may review what you own, what has changed, what worries you, and what you want to protect. It may end with next documents to gather, options to compare, or professionals to consult. It does not have to end with a decision the same day.

Guidance After the Policy Is Placed

The relationship should not end when an application is submitted or a policy is delivered. Clients may need help understanding delivery documents, reviewing beneficiaries, remembering why the policy was chosen, and knowing when to revisit the plan. Service matters because life changes after the first decision.

Price Services Group can help clients return to the plan after a new child, home purchase, divorce, job change, business event, retirement decision, health diagnosis, or caregiving change. The review may confirm that the current plan still fits, or it may identify updates worth considering.

This ongoing guidance is part of making the book's education practical. The reader should not feel pushed. The reader should feel invited into a clearer conversation with someone who can help them sort the details.

From Education to a Personal Review

This book gives language for the conversation, but it cannot know your health, budget, family structure, debts, employer benefits, business obligations, existing policies, or retirement income plan. That is why the next step is a review, not a guess.

In a personalized conversation, Kayla can help look at what you already have, explain what it appears to do, identify questions for the carrier or employer, and discuss whether new coverage or an update should be considered. The conversation may include term life, whole life, universal life, indexed universal life education, final expense, mortgage protection, children's coverage, living benefits, long-term care planning, retirement income planning, safe money strategies, beneficiary planning, legacy planning, or business owner protection.

The invitation is intentionally soft because the decision is personal. If the book helped you notice a gap, bring that note to the review. Clarity is a strong first step.

Why a Review Is Not a Sales Script

A review with Price Services Group should feel different from a product pitch. The conversation begins with the client's life: family, work, debts, retirement goals, business responsibilities, health considerations, and current coverage. From there, Kayla can help explain whether the existing plan appears aligned or whether there are gaps worth discussing.

Sometimes the review may lead to a new application. Sometimes it may lead to updating beneficiaries, requesting in-force illustrations, checking employer benefits, revisiting a business agreement, or consulting another professional. That is still valuable work. A trusted guide helps the client understand the next right step, even when the next step is simply getting better information.

A Final Note on Bringing the Question Forward

Many readers will finish this chapter with one or two questions that feel more important than the rest. That is enough. A protection review does not require the client to arrive with a finished answer. It works best when the client brings the concern that will not leave them alone: a spouse who would need income, a child who depends on care, an older policy nobody understands, a business obligation, a mortgage, a beneficiary question, or a retirement income worry.

When that concern is named, the review can become specific. Kayla can help look at the existing coverage, explain what is clear, identify what needs confirmation, and discuss whether the plan still matches the family's life. The goal is not to make every chapter a separate project. The goal is to turn awareness into one thoughtful next conversation.

Reflection for Your Notes

As you think about how price services group can help, write down what feels settled and what still feels unclear. A protection review is not about proving that you already know the answer. It is about bringing the right questions into the room so the next step is based on your life, your people, your budget, and your priorities.

Chapter 18: About the Author

The Real-Life Reason

Kayla Price brings a client-centered approach to conversations many families have been avoiding. Her work through Price Services Group is grounded in the belief that people deserve clear explanations, respectful pacing, and guidance that begins with their actual life.

In a healthy planning conversation, the person behind the guidance is the starting point. The goal is not to make anyone anxious or to make a product sound perfect. The goal is to understand what the coverage is supposed to protect, how long that need may last, and what tradeoffs are reasonable for the household.

Protection planning is not about fear. It is about giving the people you love more room to breathe if income, health, debt, business responsibilities, or family needs change unexpectedly.

A policy may be part of the answer, but the policy should follow the purpose. Clear goals make the product conversation calmer, more useful, and easier to review over time.

Plain English First

At its simplest, about the author is about helping people feel seen, informed, and protected. That does not mean every solution is simple. It means the purpose can be stated in ordinary language before the details begin.

Life insurance products are contracts, so premiums, underwriting, riders, exclusions, limitations, state availability, and policy terms all matter. The details should support the family goal instead of overwhelming it.

Some coverage is designed to last for a specific period. Some coverage is designed to last longer if premiums are paid and the policy stays in force. Some policies may build cash value. Some

may include riders that can help during qualifying illness events. Some products are built for protection only, while others may cross into retirement income, safe money, or legacy conversations.

Clients often come in thinking insurance is confusing or intimidating. Kayla's role is to make the conversation clearer and more human.

How This Can Show Up

In an early conversation, it is normal not to know which type of coverage belongs in the discussion. The review should begin with the need, then narrow the options from there.

The better question is not simply what can be purchased today. The better question is what problem the coverage is supposed to solve and how the family would actually use it later.

One common misunderstanding is that professional guidance has to feel cold or complicated. This belief can cause people to either delay planning or overcorrect with a decision that does not fit.

A Common Misread

Another misunderstanding is that about the author can be judged by one feature alone. People may focus only on premium, only on cash value, only on the death benefit, only on a rider, or only on a story they heard from someone else. Those details matter, but they need context.

Another common mistake is assuming the planning is finished once a policy is placed. Life changes, employer benefits change, beneficiaries become outdated, and some policies need attention to stay aligned with the original goal.

What people often overlook with about the author is the family conversation around it. Someone may need to know where documents are kept, who to call, what the intended purpose is, and whether there are special family dynamics to consider.

The Quiet Details

Ownership and beneficiary choices deserve careful attention. The policy owner controls the contract, the insured is the person covered, and the beneficiary receives the death benefit if the policy pays.

Timing also matters. Waiting can affect insurability, premium, and available options, while moving too quickly can create regret if the policy does not match the goal.

A protection review usually looks at personal goals, family concerns, practical next steps, and ongoing support. It may also compare existing coverage with current goals and identify gaps that are not obvious from policy pages alone.

What an Advisor Looks For

A review may include income replacement, final expenses, mortgage protection, children, aging parents, business obligations, retirement timing, health considerations, and beneficiary updates.

The review should also ask what you do not want. Some people want temporary low-cost coverage, some want lifelong protection, some want to explore cash value carefully, and some want to avoid complexity.

If this sounds like your situation, mark the section and bring your questions to a protection review.

In Short

The main lesson of this chapter is that about the author should be discussed with patience and context. A policy is only useful when it supports the real-life purpose behind it.

There is no single answer that fits every family. The right conversation considers need, time horizon, budget, health, product design, and future review.

As you continue, keep asking one simple question: what would this coverage help my family preserve, avoid, or complete?

A Soft Step Forward

The next chapter turns to annual update note, continuing the same theme: protection planning works best when the product discussion follows the human need.

A Client-Centered Voice

Kayla's role is to make planning language easier to understand and to help clients feel respected while they sort through important decisions. Through Price Services Group, L.L.C., she works to create conversations where education comes before pressure and where each client's family, business, budget, and future are treated as personal.

Readers who recognize themselves in these chapters are encouraged to bring their questions into a review instead of trying to solve every decision alone.

Why the Work Matters

Families often arrive at protection conversations carrying more than paperwork. They may be carrying grief from a past loss, confusion from old policies, worry about children, responsibility for parents, or pressure from business ownership. Kayla's work is to meet those concerns with clarity rather than overwhelm.

Price Services Group, L.L.C. is positioned as a guide for people who want to understand their choices before making them. The work is educational, practical, and personal. It is not about promising that one product can solve every problem. It is about helping clients ask better questions and make decisions with more confidence.

Reflection for Your Notes

As you think about about the author, write down what feels settled and what still feels unclear. A protection review is not about proving that you already know the answer. It is about bringing the right questions into the room so the next step is based on your life, your people, your budget, and your priorities.

Bring This Book to Your Review

Bring this book with you to your protection review appointment. If you marked pages, wrote questions, or circled sections that felt important, we can use those notes to make the conversation more personal and productive.

Chapter 19: Annual Update Note

This 2026 edition is intended to be reviewed annually. Life insurance needs, beneficiaries, coverage amounts, health status, policy performance, premium obligations, business responsibilities, debts, and family goals can change.

A policy that once fit well may need to be reviewed after a marriage, divorce, birth, adoption, home purchase, job change, business event, retirement decision, health change, caregiving change, or death in the family.

Annual Review Checklist

Each year, consider reviewing:

- ☐ Current life insurance policies and beneficiary designations
- ☐ Coverage amounts and family income needs
- ☐ Mortgage, debt, and final expense needs
- ☐ Policy premiums, lapse risk, policy loans, and cash value activity
- ☐ Living benefits, chronic illness riders, and long-term care-related rider language

Children/grandchildren coverage goals

- ☐ Business owner, key person, and buy-sell funding needs
- ☐ Retirement income, survivor income, and legacy goals
- ☐ Booking link and contact information
- ☐ Disclaimer and product/guarantee language

Final Thought

The annual review is a way of keeping promises current. It helps the plan grow with the family instead of becoming a document from a life that no longer exists.

Price Services Group, L.L.C. | Where You Matter | priceservicesgroup.com

Life Insurance / Life & Retirement Planning Appointments: https://host.safemsngr.com/widget/bookings/psglifeandretirementplan